THE
ECONOMICS
OF
DISCRIMINATION

Economics Research Studies of the Economics Research Center of the University of Chicago

Studies in the Quantity Theory of Money
MILTON FRIEDMAN, *Editor*

The Economics of Discrimination
GARY S. BECKER

THE
ECONOMICS
OF
DISCRIMINATION

Gary S. Becker

Second Edition

THE UNIVERSITY OF CHICAGO PRESS
CHICAGO & LONDON

ISBN: 0-226-04115-8 (clothbound); 0-226-04116-6 (paperbound)
Library of Congress Catalog Card Number: 73-157422

THE UNIVERSITY OF CHICAGO PRESS, CHICAGO 60637

The University of Chicago Press, Ltd., London

The second edition is dedicated to the memory of my wife, Doria Slote Becker, who died shortly before it appeared. From the time that we discussed some preliminary ideas on discrimination during our first meeting in 1953 as we strolled through Central Park until the very end she encouraged my work and aspirations.

We have lost a gentle and sensitive person.

Contents

List of Tables

Introduction to the Second Edition

Any author who receives a request from his publisher for a second edition of his book is pleased, especially if the request comes almost fifteen years after publication of what was essentially a doctoral dissertation. I confess, however, to a special pleasure because the growing interest in the book vindicates the Department of Economics of the University of Chicago, whose proposal that it be published in the series Economic Research Studies met with strong opposition. Some readers asserted that economics is not relevant in analyzing racial discrimination against minorities; others, more mildly, that the economic theory I use is not relevant; and others, milder still, that I omit too many non-economic considerations. Only the strong support of the Economics Department backed up by the confidence of the publishers in the judgment of the department overcame the opposition.

Initial reactions to the publication of *The Economics of Discrimination* supported the opposition in several ways. It was reviewed in only a few of the major economic journals.[1] Moreover, practically no studies of discrimination by economists appeared during the first five years after publication.[2]

On the other hand, many journals oriented to sociologists and

1. It was, however, generally favorably reviewed: see the reviews in the *American Economic Review* (June 1958), *Journal of the American Statistical Association* (December 1955), and *Southern Economic Journal* (April 1958). For an unfavorable review, see the *Industrial and Labor Relations Review* (December 1958).

2. The one major exception is the important article by A. A. Alchian and R. A. Kessel, "Competition, Monopoly, and the Pursuit of Pecuniary Gain," in *Aspects of Labor Economics* (Princeton: Princeton University Press, 1962).

1

other noneconomists reviewed it favorably.[3] Most importantly, the study of discrimination against minorities is presently attracting many economists: a growth in sales of the book after 1962 has been accompanied by an outpouring of articles and books by economists on minorities, especially Negroes, that is continuing to accelerate rather than abate.

Since the first edition has developed an independent life, its text is essentially left intact aside from the correction of typographical errors; I have not tried to eliminate the errors in substance or to clarify the excessively brief or the obscure passages. Instead I incorporate separately, as addenda to various chapters, three discussions of discrimination that I published after the first edition appeared.

The treatment of discrimination by trade unions in the first edition is inadequate, especially considering the importance of unions in the labor market. I did claim that "the analysis has several implications for discrimination in unionized markets," and urged a study of "the relative amount of employee discrimination in unionized and competitive labor markets" because "too often the word has been taken for the deed; that is, union pronouncements have been considered synonomous with union behavior." I clearly meant that actual union discrimination is substantially greater than that admitted in the public statements of many national union leaders. Reprinted as an addendum to chapter 4 is an analysis of union discrimination published in 1959. It explains why unions often strongly discriminate, a discrimination that has been well publicized in recent years as Negroes and other minorities have tried to gain admission to different craft unions.

Chapter 8 demonstrates that market discrimination against nonwhites apparently increases as their education and other training increases. Since I forecast an increase in their education relative to that of whites, which has occurred, I conclude that "it is important

3. See, for example, the reviews in *American Journal of Sociology* (March 1958), *Social Forces* (December 1958), *American Sociological Review* (February 1958), *Social Problems* (Winter 1958–59), *Library Journal* (August 1957), or *Social Studies* (October 1958).

to investigate the cause of the greater market discrimination against older and better-educated non-whites." As a by-product of a subsequent analysis of human capital, I considered further the relation between market discrimination and education; this analysis is presented as an addendum to chapter 8. The relatively small market discrimination against Negro male college graduates in the South, for example, is explained by the concentration of these graduates in professions like medicine or dentistry, where they can cater to a Negro clientele.

The calculations in chapter 9 of the absolute and relative occupational position of Negro males during the first fifty years of the twentieth century had more impact than any other empirical materials in the book.[4] In response to a critical comment on the method used, I published a brief elaboration and defense that also included a calculation of the change during the 1950s. This is presented as an addendum to chapter 9.

I will use the rest of this introduction to comment on several additional developments since publication of the first edition. Members of a minority group can suffer from relatively high unemployment either because they are concentrated in activities that are especially prone to unemployment, or because they are less employed in each activity. Discrimination would be responsible for their high unemployment to the extent that it was responsible either for their distribution by activity or for their greater unemployment within each activity. Discrimination could not be responsible for the latter, however, if the wage rates of minority members were sufficiently lower than those of majority members in the same activity to incorporate fully the tastes for discrimination against minorities. For then firms would have equal incentive to hire or lay off members of both groups.

Although unemployment was largely ignored in the first edition, I was aware of this important implication of the analysis, and included in my suggestions for future research the statement, "It

4. A fuller analysis that also includes females has been published by D. L. Hiestand in *Economic Growth and Employment Opportunities for Minorities* (New York: Columbia University Press, 1964).

would also be interesting to determine whether the traditionally greater unemployment of non-whites than of whites is consistent with the analysis presented here." A few calculations I had made indicated that most, but not all, of the high unemployment of non-whites resulted from their concentration in occupations that are prone to unemployment.

More intensive calculations since then, especially by Harry Gilman,[5] indicate that less than half of the greater unemployment of non-whites results from greater unemployment within an occupation. One difficulty with attributing this part to discrimination against non-whites (which is contrary to the implications of our theory) is that the differences between the unemployment rates of non-whites and whites within an occupation are apparently greater in the North than in the South,[6] although discrimination against non-whites is much greater in the South (see my chapter 8). Instead of discrimination, Gilman attributes the greater unemployment of non-whites within an occupation to the effects of minimum wages, unemployment compensation, and trade-union policies, but he does not have much evidence. No one has yet provided an explanation that is consistent, among other things, with the North-South difference.[7]

In estimating the quantitative importance of economic discrimination against members of a minority group, one needs to know what their earnings would be in the absence of different kinds of discrimination. Unfortunately, not much evidence is usually available, and somewhat arbitrary assumptions have to be made. For example, I assume in chapter 8 that white and non-white males of the same age and years of schooling would earn the same amount

5. See his "Economic Discrimination and Unemployment," *American Economic Review* (December 1965), and "The White/Non-White Unemployment Differential" in *Human Resources in the Urban Economy*, ed. M. Perlman (Baltimore: Johns Hopkins Press, 1963).

6. Ibid.

7. The *Journal of Political Economy* (June 1968) did include the North-South difference in the relative unemployment of non-whites in its "Puzzles and Problems" section, but no one has yet proposed a solution (although see the remarks in the June 1969 issue by M. J. Greenwald).

without market discrimination. Others have assumed that persons of the same IQ, suitably adjusted for cultural differences, would earn the same amount without discrimination of any kind.

The estimates in recent years of the actual productivities of different groups can sometimes be used to determine what earnings would be without market discrimination. Probably the development since the first edition of a systematic analysis of investment in human capital has the most significance for the study of economic discrimination. If members of a minority group were, on the average, as able as members of a majority group, lower earnings of the former can be said to result from a combination of less investment in human capital and discrimination against their capital.

For example, the lower quality education received by non-whites compared to that received by whites apparently explains some, but far from all, of the difference in earnings between non-whites and whites with the same years of schooling.[8] Recent work indicates that the rise in earnings with age after a person enters the labor force is primarily due to on-the-job training, learning, and other post-school investments in human capital.[9] Some, perhaps most, of the decline in the relative earnings of non-whites with age is the result of smaller post-school investments, perhaps because of discrimination in their access to these investments. The discussion in chapter 8 of discrimination against non-whites by age and schooling needs to be systematically reconsidered from the viewpoint of investment in human capital; the addendum to the chapter and other studies[10] are only a small step in this direction.

8. In the addendum to chapter 8 mentioned earlier I show not only that the amount spent per student in colleges attended by non-whites has been significantly lower than the amount spent in those attended by whites, but also that the rate of return from colleges has been lower for non-whites. Also see the study by Finis Welch of incomes in the rural South ("Labor-Market Discrimination: An Interpretation of Income Differences in the Rural South," *Journal of Political Economy* [June 1967]).

9. See, for example, J. Mincer, "The Distribution of Earnings," *Journal of Economic Literature* (March 1970).

10. See, for example, J. Mincer, "On the Job Training: Costs, Returns, and Some Implications," *Journal of Political Economy* (Supplement, October 1962).

The application of international trade theory to the analysis of discrimination against minorities (in chapter 2) is the theoretical innovation in the first edition that has had the greatest influence. I showed that while both minorities and majorities gain from "trading" (i.e., from working with members of the other group rather than just with each other), the gain usually is especially great for minorities. This conclusion was used to evaluate the economic effects of Marcus Garvey's "back to Africa" movement in the twenties, and the enforced economic segregation of American Indians. It has since been used with insight to evaluate the effects of the new separatism preached by some militant advocates of Black Power.[11]

I also showed that if, say, the majority had "tastes for discrimination" against working with the minority, "trade" would be reduced, and thus so would the money income of the minority and the net income (i.e., the income net of the psychic costs of working with the minority) of the majority. Since whites are numerically and economically much more important than non-whites in the United States, the gains from "trade" are much greater for non-whites; therefore, discrimination lowers their incomes by a relatively large percentage. On the other hand, in a country like South Africa where non-whites are so numerous, the net incomes of both groups tend to be significantly reduced by tastes for discrimination.

I was well aware from optimal tariff and general monopoly theory that a reduction in trade could increase the *money* incomes of say the majority group, but I considered this irrelevant if trade were reduced because of tastes for discrimination. It would become relevant if trade were reduced because of collective action by various members of the majority to benefit themselves at the expense of others, including the minority. These actions include price discrimination by firms with monopsonistic power in labor markets, restrictions on entry by strong trade unions, and the use of government power to further various interests.

In the addendum to chapter 4 I consider the effects of trade union

11. See Albert and Roberta Wohlstetter, " 'Third Worlds' Abroad and at Home," *Public Interest* (Winter, 1969).

restrictions on the employment of minorities. The most important and pervasive influence, however, clearly has been government action. Early in the twentieth century the government of South Africa already restricted the employment of blacks in mines—largely, it should be added, at the urging of the union of white miners. One need only note further the government harassment of Chinese merchants in Indonesia and Southeast Asia, the expulsion of Indian merchants from parts of Africa, the confiscation of some property of Japanese Americans in the United States during World War II, the restrictions legislated against Negroes in various southern states, the limited amount of public education available to Jews in eastern Europe for several centuries, or the government-imposed Apartheid in South Africa.

Of course, as demonstrated in chapter 5, minorities can often use the government to protect themselves and even to further their own interests. Witness the passage of local, state, and federal fair-employment laws in recent years,[12] the open-admissions policies of various public colleges, or the government-imposed "Philadelphia Plan" to increase the employment of minorities in the building industry.

The first edition paid only limited attention to the economic effects on minorities of collective action, and the addendum to chapter 4 on trade unions is only a small step toward a full analysis. Unfortunately, moreover, not many studies since then have dealt with it, although recently the view has been revived that majorities discriminate in order to raise their money incomes at the expense of minorities.[13] In addition to government and trade union discrimination, collusion in the non-union private sector is also stressed, even

12. In an excellent analysis of the effects of state laws, William Landes shows that they apparently have raised both the earnings and the unemployment of non-whites. See his "Economics of Fair Employment Laws," *Journal of Political Economy* (August 1968).

13. Two of the better known studies are by Anne O. Krueger, "The Economics of Discrimination," *Journal of Political Economy* (October 1963), and Lester C. Thurow, *Poverty and Discrimination* (Brookings Institution, 1969), especially chap. 7. I say "revived" because this view pervades the Marxist-inspired literature (see my discussion in chapter 2, section 2).

though no one has shown how thousands of firms and millions of workers are able to conspire successfully against minorities. (See my comments in chapter 8, section 1.) Our ignorance of the scope and incidence of collective action against minorities is perhaps the most important remaining gap in the analysis of the economic position of minorities.

Although our understanding of the economic effects of discrimination has increased significantly since the mid-fifties, I hope it increases so rapidly in the future that the materials in this book become obsolete before another decade begins.

Introduction to the First Edition

One might venture the generalization that no single domestic issue has occupied more space in our newspapers in the postwar period than discrimination against minorities, and especially against Negroes. This generalization is unquestionably true of the period since the momentous decision by the Supreme Court to outlaw segregation by color in public schools. While much of the discussion has concentrated on discrimination in such non-market activities as church and school attendance and voting, there has also been considerable discussion of discrimination in the market place—in employment, housing, transportation, etc. Such discrimination has assumed importance not only because of its direct economic consequences but also because of the belief that by eliminating market discrimination one could eliminate much of the discrimination in non-market areas.

Although discrimination against Negroes in the United States receives world-wide publicity, the extent of discrimination in the market place in this country is probably much less than in almost every other country in the world. In South Africa discrimination is also based on color; the plans for "Apartheid" envisage almost complete residential segregation of whites and blacks and large-scale segregation and discrimination in other market areas. In other Commonwealth countries and in many of Great Britain's colonies there is much discrimination against colored people; but, since market discrimination by Englishmen is combined with geographical separation from England, this is often not considered "English discrimination." In most undeveloped countries there is so much discrimination against women and persons of lowly origins (e.g., the "untouchables") that this is uniformly agreed to be a major obstacle

9

to rapid economic progress. In Great Britain, France, and other western European countries there is still discrimination against persons from lower classes and in Communist countries against persons with capitalistic backgrounds. These examples should suffice to show that a study of the economic consequences of discrimination is applicable not only to the United States but to almost every country in the world.

A study of this kind could provide the information needed for wise private and public decisions. For example: (1) If discrimination against minorities increased as their relative number increased, this would at least partly explain the difference between the treatment of Negroes in the North and South and would argue against northerners treating southern discrimination as indicating a wholly alien temperament. (2) Regardless of how "equal pay for equal work" of men and women is defined, an adequate evaluation requires knowledge of its economic effects. (3) Some observers have claimed that Negroes today are no better off economically than they were thirty or forty years ago; a public policy of outlawing discrimination would be in greater demand if minorities had made little economic progress during this century. (4) As a final example, antitrust policy would be put in a new light if monopolistic enterprises were known to discriminate more than competitive enterprises.

In view of the importance of discrimination, it may seem surprising that economists have neglected its study.[1] One can only speculate about the reasons for this neglect. Other social scientists, notably the sociologists and anthropologists, by their early entrance into this field may have established it as their property; the economist here, as elsewhere, has respected the property rights of others. The inability of economists to deal in a quantitative way with nonpecuniary motives could have been a sufficient deterrent, since such motives constitute an essential aspect of discrimination in the market place. They have lacked a systematic theory with which to interpret the economic differentials between majority and minority

1. One interesting exception is the article by Donald Dewey, "Negro Employment in Southern Industry," *Journal of Political Economy*, LX (August, 1952), 279–93.

groups, a theory that could weave together discrimination toward minority groups with free choice of enterprise and occupation.

I have attempted to remedy this neglect by developing a theory of discrimination in the market place that supplements the psychologists' and sociologists' analysis of causes with an analysis of economic consequences. While even the causes are not well understood, the absence of adequate discussions of consequences is probably the most serious lacuna in the literature on the subject. This theory can be applied to "discrimination" and "nepotism" in all their diverse forms, whether the discrimination be against Negroes, Jews, women, or persons with "unpleasant" personalities or whether the nepotism be in favor of blood relatives, countrymen, or classmates, since they have in common the use of non-monetary considerations in deciding whether to hire, work with, or buy from an individual or group.

This theory is applicable not only to discrimination and nepotism in the market place but also to non-market discrimination and nepotism and, indeed, more generally to other kinds of non-pecuniary motivation as well. From this viewpoint the major contribution of the book is to develop a theory of non-pecuniary motivation and to apply it quantitatively to discrimination in the market place. It is my belief that this application will stimulate the quantitative analysis of non-pecuniary motivation in other areas.

The plan of the book is as follows. Chapter 1 sets out the basic approach and some important definitions. Chapter 2 applies the theory of international trade to the evaluation in a general way of the effect of discrimination on the incomes of different groups. Chapters 3, 4, and 5 treat separately the effects of discrimination by employers, employees, consumers, and governments on the incomes of particular factors. Among the topics considered are the relative amounts of discrimination in monopolistic and competitive industries and in unionized and competitive labor markets, the causes of residential discrimination and segregation, and the effectiveness of discrimination by competitive and complementary factors. Chapter 6 develops a theory of the joint effects of discrimination by employers, employees, consumers, and governments. This theory tells why southern industry specializes in small establishments and why Negroes prefer some occupations and industries to others.

Chapters 7, 8, and 9 consider several additional applications of the theory developed in earlier chapters, including, among other things, the causes of regional differences in market discrimination and whether discrimination against Negroes has changed over time.

I have been fortunate to receive support from two foundations and encouragement and criticism from many people. I would like to express my gratitude to the Earhart Foundation for granting me a fellowship for the academic year 1953–54; to the Sears Roebuck Foundation for making funds available for research assistance; and to W. J. Baumol, E. J. Hamilton, A. C. Harberger, D. G. Johnson, J. Marschak, F. Mosteller, T. W. Schultz, G. J. Stigler, J. Willett, and M. Zeman for helpful comments.

I am especially indebted to H. Gregg Lewis, who has generously given his time to numerous discussions of the ideas in this book. He has influenced virtually every page, so that, whatever defects may remain, the end product would have been vastly inferior without his help; to Milton Friedman, not only for his comments on several drafts of this book, but also for training in economic analysis and for continually emphasizing that economic analysis can be used for the solution of important social problems; and to my wife Doria, for her computational, typing, and literary help and for her patience and encouragement.

CHAPTER ONE

The Forces Determining Discrimination in the Market Place

In the sociopsychological literature on this subject one individual is said to discriminate against (or in favor of) another if his behavior toward the latter is not motivated by an "objective" consideration of fact.[1] It is difficult to use this definition in distinguishing a violation of objective facts from an expression of tastes or values. For example, discrimination and prejudice are not usually said to occur when someone prefers looking at a glamorous Hollywood actress rather than at some other woman; yet they are said to occur when he prefers living next to whites rather than next to Negroes. At best calling just one of these actions "discrimination" requires making subtle and rather secondary distinctions.[2] Fortunately, it is not necessary to get involved in these more philosophical issues. It is possible to give an unambiguous definition of discrimination in the market place and yet get at the essence of what is usually called discrimination.

1. Many references can be cited for definitions of this kind. In a discussion of the problems involved in defining prejudice, Gordon Allport arrives at this definition: "Ethnic prejudice is an antipathy based upon a faulty and inflexible generalization" (see his *The Nature of Prejudice* [Cambridge, Mass.: Addison-Wesley Press, 1955], p. 9).

2. The distinction drawn by Allport and others is that those discriminating against Negroes give "erroneous" answers to various questions about Negroes, while those asked about Hollywood actresses do not. Let us waive the problem of determining whether some answers are erroneous and probe this distinction from another direction. Suppose that the answers given about Negroes violate no known facts, while those given about Hollywood actresses are in blatant conflict with the facts. Would persons drawing this distinction now agree that the preference for whites is not, and that for actresses is, discrimination?

13

1. THE ANALYTICAL FRAMEWORK

Money, commonly used as a measuring rod, will also serve as a measure of discrimination. If an individual has a "taste for discrimination," he must act *as if* he were willing to pay something, either directly or in the form of a reduced income, to be associated with some persons instead of others. When actual discrimination occurs, he must, in fact, either pay or forfeit income for this privilege. This simple way of looking at the matter gets at the essence of prejudice and discrimination.

Social scientists tend to organize their discussion of discrimination in the market place according to their disciplines. To the sociologist, different levels of discrimination against a particular group are associated with different levels of social and physical "distance" from that group or with different levels of socioeconomic status; the psychologist classifies individuals by their personality types, believing that this is the most useful organizing principle. The breakdown used here is most familiar to the economist and differs from both of these: all persons who contribute to production in the same way, e.g., by the rent of capital or the sale of labor services, are put into one group, with each group forming a separate "factor of production." The breakdown by economic productivity turns out to be a particularly fruitful one, since it emphasizes phenomena that have long been neglected in literature on discrimination.

By using the concept of a *discrimination coefficient* (this will often be abbreviated to "DC"), it is possible to give a definition of a "taste for discrimination" that is parallel for different factors of production, employers, and consumers. The *money* costs of a transaction do not always completely measure *net* costs, and a DC acts as a bridge between money and net costs. Suppose an *employer* were faced with the money wage rate π of a particular factor; he is assumed to act as if $\pi(1 + d_i)$ were the *net* wage rate, with d_i as his DC against this factor. An *employee*, offered the money wage rate π_j for working with this factor, acts as if $\pi_j(1 - d_j)$ were the net wage rate, with d_j as his DC against this factor. A *consumer*, faced with a unit money price of p for the commodity "produced" by this factor, acts as if the net price were $p(1 + d_k)$, with d_k as his DC against this factor. In all three instances a DC gives the percentage by which either money costs or money returns are changed in going from money to net magnitudes: the employer uses it to estimate his net wage costs, the employee his net wage rate, and the consumer the net price of a commodity.

A DC represents a non-pecuniary element in certain kinds of transactions, and it is positive or negative, depending upon whether the non-pecuniary element is considered "good" or "bad." Discrimination is commonly associated with *disutility* caused by contact with some individuals, and this interpretation is followed here. Since this implies that d_i, d_j, and d_k are all greater than zero, to the employer this coefficient represents a non-monetary cost of production, to the employee a non-monetary cost of employment, and to the consumer a non-monetary cost of consumption.[3] "Nepotism" rather than "discrimination" would occur if they were less than zero, and they would then represent non-monetary *returns* of production, employment, and consumption to the employer, employee, and consumer, respectively.

The quantities πd_i, $\pi_j d_j$, and $p d_k$ are the exact money equivalents of these non-monetary costs; for given wage rates and prices, these money equivalents are larger, the larger d_i, d_j, and d_k are. Since a DC can take on any value between zero and plus infinity, tastes for discrimination can also vary continuously within this range. This quantitative representation of a taste for discrimination provides the means for empirically estimating the quantitative importance of discrimination.

3. Allport makes a distinction between negative and positive prejudice that is identical with my distinction between a taste for discrimination and a taste for nepotism. He agrees that negative prejudice is usually the motivating force behind behavior considered to be discriminatory (*op. cit.*, pp. 6 and 7). He asserts later (p. 25) that "we hear so little about love [positive] prejudice" because "prejudices of this sort create no social problem." In this he is mistaken, since the social and economic implications of positive prejudice or nepotism are very similar to those of negative prejudice or discrimination.

2. TASTES FOR DISCRIMINATION

The magnitude of a taste for discrimination differs from person to person, and many investigators have directed their energies toward discovering the variables that are most responsible for these differences. I also attempt to isolate and estimate the quantitative importance of some of these variables; the following discussion briefly describes several variables that receive attention in subsequent chapters.

The discrimination by an individual against a particular group (to be called N) depends on the social and physical distance between them and on their relative socioeconomic status. If he works with N in production, it may also depend on their substitutability in production. The relative number of N in the society at large also may be very important: it has been argued that an increase in the numerical importance of a minority group increases the prejudice against them, since the majority begins to fear their growing power; on the other hand, some argue that greater numbers bring greater knowledge and that this leads to a decline in prejudice. Closely related to this variable are the frequency and regularity of "contact" with N in different establishments and firms.

According to our earlier definition, if someone has a "taste for discrimination," he must act *as if* he were willing to forfeit income in order to avoid certain transactions; it is necessary to be aware of the emphasis on the words "as if." An employer may refuse to hire Negroes solely because he erroneously underestimates their economic efficiency. His behavior is discriminatory not because he is prejudiced against them but because he is ignorant of their true efficiency. Ignorance may be quickly eliminated by the spread of knowledge, while a prejudice (i.e., preference) is relatively independent of knowledge.[4] This distinction is essential for understanding the motivation of many organizations, since they either explicit-

4. Many prejudiced people often erroneously answer questions about groups they discriminate against; their "ignorance" about these groups, however, is of secondary importance for understanding and combatting their discrimination, since their behavior is independent of all attempts to give them the facts. For a similar observation see *ibid.*, chap. i.

ly or implicitly assume that discrimination can be eliminated by a wholesale spread of knowledge.[5]

Since a taste for discrimination incorporates both prejudice and ignorance, the amount of knowledge available must be included as a determinant of tastes. Another proximate determinant is geographical and chronological location: discrimination may vary from country to country, from region to region within a country, from rural to urban areas within a region, and from one time period to another. Finally, tastes may differ simply because of differences in personality.

3. MARKET DISCRIMINATION

Suppose there are two groups, designated by W and N, with members of W being perfect substitutes in production for members of N. In the absence of discrimination and nepotism and if the labor market were perfectly competitive, the equilibrium wage rate of W would equal that of N. Discrimination could cause these wage rates to differ; the *market discrimination coefficient* between W and N (this will be abbreviated to "MDC") is defined as the proportional difference between these wage rates. If π_w and π_n represent the equilibrium wage rates of W and N, respectively, then

$$\mathrm{MDC} = \frac{\pi_w - \pi_n}{\pi_n}.$$

If W and N are imperfect substitutes, they may receive different wage rates even in the absence of discrimination. A more general definition of the MDC sets it equal to the difference between the ratio of W's to N's wage rate with and without discrimination.[6] In the special case of perfect substitutes, this reduces to the simpler definition given previously, because π_w^0 would equal π_n^0.

5. Some advertisements are primarily devoted to spreading knowledge, while others are aimed at changing preferences or prejudices by creating pleasant, although logically irrelevant, associations with their products. Likewise, some organizations try to change tastes for discrimination by creating unpleasant, although similarly irrelevant, associations with discrimination.

6. That is, $\mathrm{MDC} = \pi_w/\pi_n - \pi_w^0/\pi_n^0$, where π_w^0 and π_n^0 are the equilibrium wage rates without discrimination.

It should be obvious that the magnitude of the MDC depends on the magnitude of individual DC's. Unfortunately, it is often implicitly assumed that it depends *only* on them; the arguments proceed as if a knowledge of the determinants of tastes was sufficient for a complete understanding of market discrimination. This procedure is erroneous; many variables in addition to tastes take prominent roles in determining market discrimination, and, indeed, tastes sometimes play a minor part. The abundant light thrown on these other variables by the tools of economic analysis has probably been the major insight gained from using them.

The MDC does depend in an important way on each individual's DC; however, merely to use some measure of the average DC does not suffice. The complete distribution of DC's among individuals must be made explicit because the size of the MDC is partly related to individual *differences* in tastes. It also depends on the relative importance of competition and monopoly in the labor and product markets, since this partly determines the weight assigned by the market to different DC's. The economic and quantitative importance of N was mentioned as one determinant of tastes for discrimination; this variable is also an independent determinant of market discrimination. This independent effect operates through the number of N relative to W and the cost of N per unit of output relative to the total cost per unit of output. Both may be important, although for somewhat different reasons, in determining the weight assigned by the market to different DC's. Reorganizing production through the substitution of one factor for another is a means of avoiding discrimination; the amount of substitution available is determined by the production function.

The MDC is a direct function of these variables and an indirect function of other variables through their effect on tastes. Our knowledge of the economic aspects of discrimination will be considered satisfactory only when these relationships are known exactly. In subsequent chapters I present the results of my own attempts to close some gaps in this knowledge.

CHAPTER TWO

Effective Discrimination

An MDC between any two groups can be defined for a particular labor or capital market or for all markets combined; in the latter, interest would center on the effect of discrimination on the total incomes of these groups. For example, discrimination by whites presumably reduces the income of Negroes, but how does it affect their own incomes? Many writers have asserted that discrimination in the market place by whites is in their own self-interest; i.e., it is supposed to raise their incomes. If this were correct, it would be in the self-interest of Negroes to "retaliate" against whites by discriminating against them, since this should raise Negro incomes. If, on the other hand, discrimination by whites reduces their own incomes as well, is the percentage reduction in their incomes greater or less than that in Negro incomes? It is an implicit assumption of most discussions that minority groups like Negroes usually suffer more from market discrimination than do majority groups like whites, but no one has isolated the fundamental structural reasons why this is so. It is shown in the following that discrimination by any group W reduces their own incomes as well as N's, and thus retaliation by N makes it worse for N rather than better. It is also shown why minorities suffer much more from discrimination than do majorities.

1. THE MODEL

New insights are gained and the analysis made simpler if the discussion is phrased in terms of trade between two "societies," one inhabited solely by N, the other by W. Government and monopolies are ignored for the present, as the analysis is confined to perfectly competitive societies. Since our emphasis here is on the over-all incomes of W and N, the multiplicity of factors of production will also be ignored, and the discussion will be confined to two homogeneous factors in each society—labor and capital—with each unit of labor and capital in N being a perfect substitute in *production* for each unit of labor and capital in W. These societies do not "trade" commodities but factors of production used in producing commodities. Each society finds it advantageous to "export" its relatively abundant factors: W exports capital, and N labor. The amount of labor exported by N at a given rate of exchange of labor for capital is the difference between the total amount of labor in N and the amount used "domestically"; the amount of capital exported by W is derived in a similar manner.

The following conditions would be satisfied in a full equilibrium with no discrimination: (*a*) payment to each factor would be independent of whether it was employed with N or W; (*b*) the price of each product would be independent of whether it was produced by N or W; and (*c*) the unit payment to each factor would equal its marginal value product. If members of W develop a desire to discriminate against labor and capital owned by N, they become willing to forfeit money income in order to avoid working with N. This taste for discrimination reduces the net return[1] that W capital can receive by combining with N labor, and this leads to a reduction in the amount of W capital exported. Since this, in turn, reduces the income that N labor can receive by combining with W capital, less N labor is also exported. In the new equilibrium, then, less labor and capital are exported by N and W, respectively. It can be shown that this change in resource allocation reduces the equi-

1. If W wants to discriminate, exported capital must receive a higher equilibrium money return than domestically used capital, to compensate for working with N labor. However, if all W has the same taste for discrimination, the equilibrium net return must be the same for all W capital. Net and money returns to domestic capital are identical, since there are no psychic costs to working with W labor; therefore, the eqilibrium money return to domestic capital can be used as the equilibrium net return to all W capital. The money and net returns to all W labor are the same, since it works only with W capital.

librium net incomes of both N and W.[2] Since discrimination by W hurts W as well as N, it cannot be a subtle means by which W augments its net command of economic goods.[3]

2. DISCRIMINATION AND CAPITALISTS

Although the aggregate net incomes of W and N are reduced by discrimination, all factors are not affected in the same way: the return to W capital and N labor decreases, but the return to W labor and N capital actually increases. There is a remarkable agreement in the literature on the proposition that capitalists from the dominant group are the major beneficiaries of prejudice and discrimination in a competitive capitalistic economic system.[4] If W is considered to represent whites or some other dominant group, the fallacious nature of this proposition becomes clear, since discrimina-

2. See the appendix to this chapter.

3. If we compare discrimination with tariffs, we find that, although some of their effects are similar, other effects are quite different. Discrimination always decreases both societies' net incomes, while a tariff of the appropriate size can, as Bickerdike long ago pointed out, increase the levying society's net income. A tariff operates by driving a wedge between the price a society pays for imported goods and the price each individual member pays; it does not create any distinction between net income and total command over goods. Discrimination does create such a distinction and does not drive a wedge between private and social prices. Discrimination has more in common with transportation costs than with tariffs.

4. Saenger, a psychologist, said: "Discriminatory practices appear to be of definite advantage for the representatives of management in a competitive economic system" (*The Social Psychology of Prejudice* [New York: Harper & Bros., 1953], p. 96). Allport, another psychologist, likewise said: "We conclude, therefore, that the Marxist theory of prejudice is far too simple, even though it points a sure finger at *one* of the factors involved in prejudice, viz., rationalized self-interest of the upper classes" (*The Nature of Prejudice* [Cambridge, Mass.: Addison-Wesley Press, 1955], p. 210). Similar statements can be found in A. Rose, *The Costs of Prejudice* (Paris: UNESCO, 1951), p. 7; and throughout O. C. Cox, *Caste, Class, and Race* (Garden City: Doubleday & Co., 1948); J. Dollard, *Caste and Class in a Southern Town* (New Haven: Yale University Press, 1937); C. McWilliams, *A Mask for Privilege: Anti-Semitism in America* (Boston: Little, Brown & Co., 1948); H. Aptheker, *The Negro Problem in America* (New York: International Publishers, 1946); and many other books as well.

tion *harms* W capitalists and benefits W workers. The most serious non sequitur in the mistaken analyses is the (explicit or implicit) conclusion that, if tastes for discrimination cause N laborers to receive a lower wage rate than W laborers, the difference between these wage rates must accrue as "profits" to W capitalists.[5] These profits would exist only if this wage differential resulted from price discrimination (due to monopsony power), rather than from a taste for discrimination.

3. DISCRIMINATION AND SEGREGATION

Trade between two societies is maximized when there is no discrimination, and it decreases with all increases in discrimination. Tastes for discrimination might become so large that it would no longer pay to trade; each society would be in economic isolation and would have to get along with its own resources. Since members of each society would be working only with each other, complete economic isolation would also involve *complete* economic *segregation*. More generally, since an increase in discrimination decreases trade and since a decrease in trade means an increase in economic segregation, an increase in discrimination must be accompanied by an increase in segregation.

The total MDC against N is defined as the difference between the actual ratio of the incomes of W and N and this ratio without discrimination.[6] There is "effective discrimination" against N when-

5. D. A. Wilkerson, in his Introduction to Aptheker's book, said: "Precisely this same relationship between material interests and Negro oppression exists today. . . . The per capita annual income of southern Negro tenant farmers and day laborers in 1930 was about $71, as compared with $97 for similar white workers. Multiply this difference of $26 by the 1,205,000 Negro tenants and day laborers on southern farms in 1930, and it is seen that planters 'saved' approximately $31,000,000 by the simple device of paying Negro workers less than they paid white workers" (Aptheker, *op. cit.*, p. 10).

6. Let $Y(N)$ and $Y(W)$ represent the actual incomes of N and W, and $Y_0(N)$ and $Y_0(W)$ their incomes without discrimination. The total MDC is defined as

$$\mathrm{MDC} = \frac{Y(W)}{Y(N)} - \frac{Y_0(W)}{Y_0(N)}.$$

ever this MDC is positive. If effective discrimination occurs against *N* at all levels of discrimination by *W*, the income of *N* relative to *W* must be less when completely isolated from *W* than when freely trading with *W;* under these circumstances, *N* gains more from trade than *W* does.

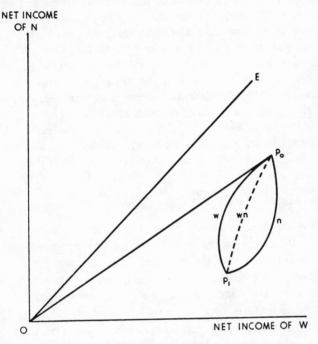

Fig. 1.—The effect of discrimination on incomes

It is proved in the appendix to this chapter that if effective discrimination occurs against *N* at all levels of discrimination by *W*, the absolute and relative income of *N* declines continuously as discrimination increases. This is shown in Figure 1, in which the horizontal axis measures *W*'s and the vertical axis *N*'s net income; p_0 represents their incomes when there is no discrimination, p_1 when there is complete segregation, and the curve $p_0 w p_1$ when there are different amounts of discrimination by *W*. We have assumed that effective discrimination always occurs against N; therefore, $p_0 w p_1$ is never above the line $o p_0$. The total MDC against N increases as discrimination increases; incomes reach a *minimum* and the total MDC a *maximum* when tastes for discrimination become sufficiently large to preclude any trade between W and N. This conclusion is very relevant to a proposal that has stimulated considerable discussion in the past, namely, that minority groups should avoid discrimination from the majority by completely segregating themselves, economically and otherwise.[7] If the minority is identified with N and the majority with W, this analysis demonstrates that complete segregation reduces the absolute and relative income of the minority and therefore increases, rather than decreases, the market discrimination against it. Effective discrimination occurs against a minority partly because it gains so much by "trading" with the majority; accordingly, complete segregation does not avoid the bad economic effects of discrimination but only multiplies them.

4. THE INCOME OF INDIANS AND NEGROES

The foregoing conclusion can be investigated empirically by comparing the incomes of two minority groups, one segregated from and the other trading with the dominant group. The American Indians are taken as a group that has been segregated from American whites (partly by choice and partly by force) and the American Negroes as a group that has been trading with these whites. Though Indians have had some economic contact with whites, they almost certainly have had less than Negroes. If, when the Negro slaves were freed, their per capita resources were no greater than the Indians' per capita resources, one can reasonably attribute some of the present difference between per capita Negro and Indian incomes to differences in their contact with whites. Data are presented in Table 1, indicating that the median Indian net income in the United States

7. In the 1920's there was a large movement, under the leadership of Marcus Garvey, to take Negroes in America back to Africa to "escape from" discrimination. This conclusion is also helpful in understanding some effects of "Apartheid."

in 1949 was only 76 per cent of the median Negro net income.[8]
Negro incomes were larger in five separate regions and urban-rural
classes, smaller in one, and the same in one. Thus, for both the
country as a whole and for smaller units, Negro incomes were substantially higher than Indian incomes in 1949.[9]

TABLE 1

MEDIAN INCOME OF INDIANS AND NEGROES IN 1950
BY REGION AND URBAN-RURAL CLASSIFICATION*

REGION	URBAN	RURAL FARM	RURAL NON-FARM	ALL
	Median Income of Negroes (Dollars)			
Northeast...........	1,623	1,050	†	....
North-central.......	1,697	560	....	....
South..............	861	431	....	....
West...............	1,524	897	....	....
United States.......	....	....	....	952
	Median Income of Indians (Dollars)			
Northeast...........	1,626	....	1,033	....
North-central.......	1,188	360	602	....
South..............	1,168	366	682	....
West...............	1,180	406	721	....
United States.......	....	....	....	725

* Source: U.S. Bureau of the Census, *Census of Population, 1950: Special
Report on Non-White Populations by Race* (Washington, D.C.: Government Printing Office, 1953), Tables 9 and 11.

† Data are not available.

8. In using money income to measure net income it is implicitly assumed that
the cost to Negroes of trading with whites is small relative to their total command over goods.

9. It is not clear that a region-urban-rural breakdown of the data is desirable, since some of the advantages of trading with whites stem from the possibility of moving to remunerative white urban areas or even to other regions.

These data might underestimate Indian male incomes if a larger proportion of
the Indian than of the Negro labor force were female, since females generally
earn less than males. However, only 20 per cent of the Indian labor force was

5. DISCRIMINATION AND ECONOMIC MINORITIES

I have shown that a necessary and sufficient condition for effective discrimination to occur against N at all levels of discrimination by W is[10]

$$\frac{Y_0(W)}{Y_0(N)} > \frac{l_n}{l_w}, \qquad (1)$$

where l_n and l_w represent the amount of labor supplied by N and W, and $Y_0(W)$ and $Y_0(N)$ represent the aggregate incomes of W and N in the absence of discrimination. If N is a numerical minority, $l_n < l_w$[11] and $c_n < c_w$,[12] where c_n and c_w represent the amount of capital supplied by N and W. Therefore

$$\frac{Y_0(W)}{Y_0(N)} > 1, \qquad (2)$$

_____

female in 1950, as against 35 per cent of the Negro labor force (see U.S. Bureau of the Census, *Census of Population, 1950: Special Report on Non-White Populations by Race* [Washington, D.C.: Government Printing Office, 1953], Tables 9 and 10). Thus median Indian male incomes were probably *less* than the 76 per cent of Negro male incomes cited in the text for 1949.

One might suspect that the Indian population had been increasing at a faster rate than the Negro, so that some of the increase in Indian income had been taken up in the form of a relatively larger population. Once again the contrary seems to be true. Estimates of the Indian population date from 1890; in that year Indian population was 3 per cent of the Negro population, and in 1950 it was 2 per cent (see U.S. Bureau of the Census, *Statistical Abstract of the United States, 1953* [Washington, D.C.: Government Printing Office, 1954], p. 38). Therefore, the Negro population has increased at a significantly faster rate than the Indian.

Nor are there very large differences in education between the two groups. The median number of years of schooling in 1950 was 6.9 for Negro males and 7.7 for Negro females; 7.3 for Indian males and 7.4 for Indian females (see U.S. Bureau of the Census, *Special Report on Non-White Populations by Race*, Table 9).

This comparison is intended to be suggestive and not conclusive. Much more detailed work is necessary to determine the income of Indians and Negroes in the late nineteenth century and to standardize these income data for 1949.

10. See the appendix to this chapter (pp. 35–37).

11. If N is a numerical minority, the amount of labor owned by $N(l_n')$ is less than that owned by $W(l_w')$. The amount supplied to the market is $l_n = a_n l_n'$ and $l_w = a_w l_w'$. If $a_n = a_w$, $l_n' < l_w'$ implies $l_n < l_w$. More generally, $l_n' < l_w'$ implies $l_n < l_w$ if, and only if, $a_n/a_w < l_w'/l_n'$. This seems like a plausible restriction and is implicit in the inferences drawn in the text.

12. N exports labor if, and only if, $l_n/l_w > c_n/c_w$. If $l_n < l_w$, then $c_n < c_w$.

and a fortiori that inequality (1) holds. Inequality (2) states that N's income is less than W's and hence that N is an economic minority. Therefore, if N is a numerical minority, it is also an economic minority, and effective discrimination must occur against it. If N is not a numerical minority, inequalities (1) and (2) no longer necessarily hold; they hold only if N is more of an economic minority than W is a numerical minority.[13]

It turns out, then, that a necessary condition for effective discrimination against N is that N be an economic minority; a sufficient condition is that N be a numerical minority; a necessary *and* sufficient condition is that N be more of an economic minority than a numerical majority. It has long been recognized that discrimination is closely connected with the minorities question, the emphasis being put on the inadequate political representation of numerical minorities. This analysis of discrimination in competitive free-enterprise societies also uses a minority-majority framework, but the concept of economic minorities is somewhat more important here than that of numerical ones. It seems reasonable that economic discrimination in competitive societies be related to economic minorities, and political discrimination to political minorities.

6. DISCRIMINATION IN THE REAL WORLD

a) *Negroes in the United States*

Only about 10 per cent of the total population of the United States is Negro; hence the amount of labor they supply is substantially less than the amount supplied by whites. Moreover, Negroes must be a net "exporter" of labor, since they clearly have more labor relative to capital than do the whites. These two conditions imply (by n. 12 and inequality [1]) that tastes for discrimination would produce—via the workings of a competitive economic system—effective discrimination against Negroes. There is evidence not only that effective discrimination occurs against Negroes but also that the total MDC is quite large. Negroes in the United States have owned an extremely small amount of capital, while

13. This statement is completely rigorous only if $a_n = a_w$.

whites have had a more balanced distribution of resources;[14] a substantial decline in the amount of white capital available to Negroes would greatly reduce the absolute and relative incomes of Negroes.

Estimates could be made of the economic loss to various groups resulting from discrimination in the market place if there were knowledge of the actual quantity of discrimination, the nature of production functions, and the amount of labor and capital supplied. A general technique for making these estimates will be illustrated by an example that also roughly indicates the magnitude of the economic loss to Negroes and whites in the United States resulting from discrimination in the market place by whites.

The production function is assumed to be of the following (Cobb-Douglas) form

$$X = kl^r c^{1-r} ,$$

with $r = \frac{2}{3}$. The amount of labor supplied by whites is taken as 9 times that supplied by Negroes, and of capital as 150 times.[15] Since units of measurement can be chosen at will, Negroes are assumed to have one unit of both labor and capital; these assumptions state that $l_n = 1$, $c_n = 1$, $l_w = 9$, and $c_w = 150$. If there were no discrimination, the incomes of Negroes and whites would be $Y_0(N) = 1.7$ and $Y_0(W) = 23.5$, and whites would export 14 units of capital; if discrimination were sufficiently large to cause complete segregation, their incomes would be $Y_1(N) = 1.0$ and $Y_1(W) = 23.2$ (see pp. 24–27). The maximum reduction in the income of Negroes is about 40 per cent; the income of whites would

14. Some mutual interaction may have occurred here, since poverty is a cause, as well as a result, of an unbalanced distribution of resources. For example, poor individuals often find it very difficult to obtain funds for investments in themselves.

15. This considers capital invested in humans as capital and not labor. If it were considered as labor, the assumption that Negro and white labor were perfect substitutes in production would be untenable, since whites have more capital invested in themselves than Negroes have. Since the number of Negroes in the labor force is about one-nineth the number of whites, the assumption that white labor is nine times that of Negro labor is reasonable if the innate capacities of whites and Negroes are roughly the same. The ratio of white to Negro capital was arrived at essentially by a guess. Our model implies that Negroes in the United States "export" unskilled labor to whites and that whites "export" capital—including skilled labor—to Negroes.

be reduced by an almost imperceptible amount. With no discrimination, Negro per capita incomes would be about 66 per cent of those of whites, and, with complete segregation, about 39 per cent of those of whites.

The actual equilibrium position falls somewhere between these two extremes. If discrimination reduces the amount of capital exported by whites by about 40 per cent, they would actually export 8 rather than 14 units of capital; Negro and white incomes would be 1.5 and 23.3, and thus per capita Negro incomes would be 57 per cent of per capita white incomes. An MDC against Negro labor can be defined as the percentage difference between actual white and Negro net wage rates; an MDC against Negro capital as the percentage difference between actual white and Negro net rents on capital. These MDC's would be $+0.21$ and -0.31, respectively; hence the return to labor would be greater for whites, and the return to capital would be greater for Negroes. White labor and Negro capital gain from discrimination, and white capital and Negro labor lose from it; but, since the net loss of Negroes is greater than that of whites, total market discrimination occurs against Negroes. Discrimination in the market place by whites reduces Negro incomes by 13 per cent, or, to put this in other words, Negro incomes would increase 16 per cent if market discrimination ceased. Discrimination reduces the incomes of whites by a negligible amount because they gain very little from trading with Negroes.

The estimated economic loss to Negroes would be greater if the production function was more capital-intensive, if white capital was larger relative to Negro capital, or if discrimination reduced the amount of capital exported by more than 40 per cent. Likewise, the estimated loss would be smaller if the opposite conditions were assumed. Inadequate knowledge of these variables makes it impossible to estimate this loss precisely, and 16 per cent is an extremely rough estimate. The economic loss to Negroes seems substantial and important, although a far cry from the loss assumed in some discussions.[16]

16. I have come across only one clear and explicit attempt to estimate the economic costs of discrimination. The technique used is clearly stated in the following paragraph:

"The results of these calculations represent a shocking reminder of the real

It is often explicitly or implicitly assumed that the total MDC against Negroes is very large (to use the terms of this study); explanations have emphasized political discrimination, class warfare, monopolies, and market imperfections. My analysis shows that none of these influences is necessary, since substantial market discrimination against Negroes in the United States could easily result from the manner in which individual tastes for discrimination allocate resources within a competitive free-enterprise framework. The United States is often considered the best example of a country using competition to determine economic values. This implies that monopolies, political discrimination, and the like, are, at most, secondary determinants of market discrimination and that individual tastes for discrimination operating within a competitive framework constitute the primary determinant.

b) Non-Whites in South Africa

In South Africa, non-whites are about 80 per cent of the total population; this is taken to mean that l_n is roughly four times l_w (see inequality [1] on p. 26). Since non-whites are a numerical majority, effective discrimination does not *necessarily* occur against them; it would occur if aggregate white net incomes were at least

---

cost of discrimination to our country in production, expressed in dollars and cents terms. We found that the average annual income of the Negro family is $1043. The average income for Whites is $3062, or roughly three times that of Negroes. And, when the difference in income is multiplied by the number of Negro family units which could add to the productive wealth of the nation, we discovered the appalling loss of four billion dollars of real wealth annually because of discrimination against Negroes alone" (see E. Roper, "The Price Business Pays," in *Discrimination and the National Welfare*, ed. R. M. MacIver [New York: Harper & Bros., 1948], p. 18).

Roper's implicit assumption that Negroes and whites would receive the same income without discrimination is a mistake: whites would receive larger incomes than Negroes because they have much more capital per capita. In the example used here, eliminating all discrimination would raise per capita Negro incomes to only 66 per cent of per capita white incomes. This mistake partly explains why Roper assumed that Negro incomes would increase by 200 per cent, this being about ten times my estimated increase. On the other hand, his implicit assumption that whites suffer a negligible economic loss is correct.

four times aggregate non-white net incomes.[17] The very crude available evidence suggests that aggregate white net incomes are much more than four times those of non-whites.[18] Therefore, tastes for discrimination in the private economic sector alone seems to have produced effective discrimination against non-whites. The South African government has been active in regulating the economic activities of non-whites. For this reason the market discrimination produced by the competitive economic sector *may* be less important than that produced by other sources; but it need not be, since it alone could be quite large.

7. DISCRIMINATION BY MINORITIES

N may discriminate, in our model, by distinguishing between W and N capital; the money return for working with W capital must be sufficient to offset the psychic costs of doing so. A general analysis incorporating discrimination by both W and N could be developed, but there is no point in going into the details of this beyond stressing one important relationship. W's net income is uniquely determined

17. Inequality (1) refers to white and non-white incomes in equilibrium without discrimination; yet the condition stated above is in terms of actual net income with discrimination. However, there is no contradiction between these statements, since this condition implies inequality (1). If there were effective discrimination against *whites*, their relative net income would be less with discrimination than without it; so that, if their actual net incomes were at least four times those of non-whites, their incomes without discrimination would also be at least four times those of non-whites. But, by inequality (1), this implies that there must be effective discrimination against non-whites rather than against whites. Consequently, if white net incomes were at least four times those of non-whites, there must be effective discrimination against non-whites.

18. See the study of native income by D. H. Houghton and D. Philcox, "Family Income and Expenditure in a Ciskei Native Reserve," *South African Journal of Economics*, XVIII (December, 1950), 418–38, and the data giving the national income of South Africa in the report of the United Nations Statistical Office, *National and per Capita Incomes in Seventy Countries, 1949* (1950). These income figures overestimate the net incomes of whites and non-whites, since the non-monetary costs of working with each other have not been netted out of the gross production figures. It is unlikely, although not impossible, that the true net incomes of whites are less than four times those of non-whites.

by the amount of capital exported; discrimination determines this amount, and the latter alone determines W's income. N's net income depends on the amount of capital imported and its own taste for discrimination. For a given amount imported, N's net income is maximized if it is indifferent between indigenous and imported capital; the greater the preference for indigenous capital, the smaller the net income. Hence, given W's net income and thus the amount of capital exported, N's net income is smaller, the greater the discrimination. Therefore, if both N and W discriminate, inequality (1) is sufficient but not necessary for effective discrimination always to occur against N; any necessary and sufficient condition would depend on the relative amount of discrimination by N. Consider Figure 1 again. The curve $p_0 n p_1$ represents the incomes of N and W for different levels of discrimination by N, and it must be below $p_0 w p_1$ at all points except p_0 and p_1. If both W and N discriminate, the point representing their incomes would be in the area bounded by $p_0 n p_1 w$; the curve $p_0 w n p_1$ summarizes a set of situations in which W discriminates more than N does.

Minority groups are often tempted to "retaliate" against discrimination from others by returning the discrimination. This is a mistake, since effective economic discrimination occurs against them, not because of the distribution of tastes but because of the distribution of resources. That is, majorities have a more balanced distribution of labor and capital than they do. Figure 1 clearly shows that, although N is hurt by W's discrimination, it is hurt even more by its own discrimination.

APPENDIX TO CHAPTER 2

Call the net (=money) return to domestic labor and capital in W, $\pi_e(W)$ and $\pi_c(W)$. In a competitive equilibrium position the return to each factor equals its marginal productivity; hence

$$\pi_c(W) = \frac{\partial f}{\partial c}(c = c_w - c_i; l = l_w) = \frac{\partial f}{\partial c}(c_w - c_i; l_w),$$

$$\pi_l(W) = \frac{\partial f}{\partial l}(c = c_w - c_i; l = l_w) = \frac{\partial f}{\partial l}(c_w - c_i; l_w),$$

where f is the production function in W; c_w and l_w are the total amount of labor and capital supplied by W; and c_t is the amount of capital exported. By footnote 1 of this chapter the equilibrium net income of W is

$$Y(W) = c_w \pi_c(W) + l_w \pi_l(W)$$

$$= c_w \frac{\partial f}{\partial c}(c_w - c_t; l_w) + l_w \frac{\partial f}{\partial l}(c_w - c_t; l_w).$$

N allocates its labor between W and N capital, with the intent of equalizing its marginal physical product in both uses. The equilibrium net income of N is

$$Y(N) = c_n \pi_c(N) + l_n \pi_l(N) = c_n \frac{\partial f'}{\partial c}(c_n + c_t; l_n)$$

$$+ l_n \frac{\partial f'}{\partial l}(c_n + c_t; l_n),$$

where f' is the production function in N, and c_n and l_n are the total amount of labor and capital supplied by N. The impact of discrimination on $Y(W)$ and $Y(N)$ could be determined by explicitly introducing tastes for discrimination; however, the analysis is simpler with another approach. An increase in discrimination by W decreases the quantity of capital exported, and therefore the latter is a monotonic function of W's taste for discrimination.

It can be shown that if f and f' are homogeneous of the first degree,

$$\frac{\partial Y(W)}{\partial c_t} > 0, \tag{A1}$$

$$\frac{\partial Y(N)}{\partial c_t} > 0, \tag{A1'}$$

and thus discrimination by W reduces the net incomes of both N and W. Inequality (A1) can be proved thus: If a function is homogeneous of the first degree, all first-order partial derivatives are homogeneous of zero degree; in particular, $\partial f/\partial c$ is homogeneous of zero degree. By Euler's theorem for homogeneous functions,

$$c \frac{\partial (\partial f / \partial c)}{\partial c} + l \frac{\partial (\partial f / \partial c)}{\partial l} \equiv 0 \,,$$

or

$$c \frac{\partial^2 f}{\partial c^2} + l \frac{\partial^2 f}{\partial l \partial c} \equiv 0 \,. \qquad (A2)$$

According to a well-known theorem on the derivative of a function of a function,

$$\frac{\partial f}{\partial c_t} \equiv \frac{\partial f}{\partial c} \frac{\partial c}{\partial c_t}.$$

Since $c = c_w - c_t$, then $\partial c / \partial c_t = -1$, and

$$\frac{\partial f}{\partial c_t} \equiv - \frac{\partial f}{\partial c}. \qquad (A3)$$

It follows from identity (A3) that

$$\frac{\partial Y (W)}{\partial c_t} \equiv l \frac{\partial^2 f}{\partial l \partial c_t} - c_w \frac{\partial^2 f}{\partial c_t^2}, \qquad (A4)$$

and from identities (A2) and (A3) that

$$c \frac{\partial^2 f}{\partial c_t^2} \equiv l \frac{\partial^2 f}{\partial l \partial c_t}. \qquad (A5)$$

By substituting identity (A5) in identity (A4), one obtains

$$\frac{\partial Y (W)}{\partial c_t} \equiv - c_t \frac{\partial^2 f}{\partial c_t^2}. \qquad (A6)$$

If there is diminishing marginal productivity, $\partial^2 f / \partial c_t^2 < 0$. Since $c_t \geq 0$, it must follow that

$$\frac{\partial Y (W)}{\partial c_t} \geq 0 \,. \qquad \text{Q.E.D.}$$

Inequality (A1′) can be proved in the same way.

By looking at the problem in a slightly different way, it is possible to acquire an intuitive understanding of this result. Suppose labor enters the United States from abroad and that some United States capital (c_t) is employed with this labor. A well-known economic theorem states that United States citizens must (economically) benefit from immigration as long as there is diminishing marginal productivity of labor, since intra-marginal immigrants raise the productivity of American capital. The net income of United States citizens is an increasing function of the amount of immigration, which can be measured by c_t, the amount of capital employed with immigrants. This discussion shows that treating discrimination as a problem in trade and migration is far from artificial, since they are closely and profoundly related.

Let us define

$$R = \frac{Y(N)}{Y(W)}.$$

Then

$$\frac{\partial R}{\partial c_t} = \frac{Y(W)[\partial Y(N)/\partial c_t] - Y(N)[\partial Y(W)/\partial c_t]}{[Y(W)]^2},$$

or, from identity (A6),

$$\frac{\partial R}{\partial c_t} = \frac{Y(W)[-c_t(\partial^2 f'/\partial c_t^2)] - Y(N)[-c_t(\partial^2 f/\partial c_t^2)]}{[Y(W)]^2}.$$

Hence

$$\frac{\partial R}{\partial c_t} \gtreqless 0 \qquad \text{as} \qquad Y(N)\frac{\partial^2 f}{\partial c_t^2} \gtreqless Y(W)\frac{\partial^2 f'}{\partial c_t^2}. \qquad \text{(A7)}$$

If f were identical with f' and if there were no discrimination, the amount of capital exported would be just sufficient to equalize the equilibrium relative supply of factors "abroad" with the relative supply at "home." That is to say,

$$\frac{c_n + \hat{c}_t}{l_n} = \frac{c_w - \hat{c}_t}{l_w},$$

or

$$l_n = bl_w,$$

and

$$c_n + \hat{c}_t = b(c_w - \hat{c}_t).$$

Since $\partial f/\partial c_t$ is homogeneous of zero degree in c and l, $\partial^2 f/\partial c_t^2$ must be homogeneous of -1 degree in c and l,

$$\frac{\partial^2 f}{\partial c_t^2}(a\,c,\,al) = \frac{1}{a}\frac{\partial^2 f}{\partial c_t^2}(c,\,l),$$

where a is any number. If $c = c_w - \hat{c}_t$, $l = l_w$, and $a = b$, it follows that

$$\frac{\partial^2 f}{\partial c_t^2}(c_n + \hat{c}_t,\,l_n) = \frac{l_w}{l_n}\frac{\partial^2 f}{\partial c_t^2}(c_w - \hat{c}_t,\,l_w).$$

Substituting this in inequality (A7) and using the assumption of diminishing marginal productivity, we get the following simple condition:

$$\frac{\partial R}{\partial c_t/\,c_t = \hat{c}_t} \gtreqless 0 \qquad \text{as} \qquad \frac{Y(N)}{Y(W)} \lesseqgtr \frac{l_w}{l_n}, \qquad \text{(A8)}$$

or

$$\frac{Y(W)}{Y(N)} \gtreqless \frac{l_n}{l_w}.$$

If in the absence of discrimination, N's relative income were less than W's relative supply of labor, a slight taste for discrimination by W would reduce N's income by a greater percentage than it would W's.

If $\partial R/(\partial c_t/c_t = \hat{c}_t) > 0$, $\partial R/\partial c_t$ would probably be greater than zero for all admissible values of c_t. For example, if

$$\frac{\partial R}{\partial c_t/\,c_t = \hat{c}_t} > 0 \qquad \text{and} \qquad \frac{\partial^3 f}{\partial c_t^3} > 0,$$

it would follow that

$$\frac{R}{c_t = \hat{c}_t - \epsilon} < \frac{R}{c_t = \hat{c}_t},$$

where ϵ is a small positive number, and

$$\frac{\partial^2 f/\,(\partial c_t^2/\,c_t = \hat{c}_t - \epsilon)}{\partial^2 f'/\,(\partial c_t^2/\,c_t = \hat{c}_t - \epsilon)} < \frac{\partial^2 f/\,(\partial c_t^2/\,c_t = \hat{c}_t)}{\partial^2 f'/\,(\partial c_t^2/\,c_t = \hat{c}_t)} = 1.$$

Accordingly, if

$$R < \frac{\partial^2 f'/\partial c_t^2}{\partial^2 f/\partial c_t^2},$$

when $c_t = \hat{c}_t$, it must a fortiori be true when $c_t = \hat{c}_t - \epsilon$. By continuing to reason along these lines, one would readily show that it must be true for all c_t.[19] This analysis is the basis for the assumption in this chapter and the rest of the appendix that an increase in discrimination by W must reduce N's net income relative to W's, if and only if

$$\frac{1}{R} = \frac{Y(W)}{Y(N) / c_t = \hat{c}_t} > \frac{l_n}{l_w}. \tag{A9}$$

If there are different tastes for discrimination among W (or N), some new problems enter the analysis; a few are mentioned now, and more are discussed in succeeding chapters. The unit money price of domestic W capital would not equal the unit net price of exported capital: capital on the margin between working with labor supplied by N and W would, of course, receive the same net return "abroad" and "domestically"; capital with smaller tastes for discrimination would find it advantageous to work with N. All capital working with W labor would receive the same net return, but capital with relatively small tastes for discrimination would receive a larger net return for working with N labor. It follows that net income as defined here would underestimate true net income, since it assumes that the net return to all capital is the same as the net return to marginal capital. The curve representing the net

19. Although production functions that are homogeneous of the first degree do not necessarily have positive third-order partial derivatives, a wide and important class of them does, e.g., all homogeneous Cobb-Douglas functions. In general, if f is homogeneous of the first degree, Euler's theorem states that

$$l \frac{\partial f}{\partial l} + c \frac{\partial f}{\partial c} \equiv X.$$

After twice differentiating this identity with respect to c, one gets

$$\frac{c \partial^3 f}{\partial c^3} + \frac{\partial^2 f}{\partial c^2} + \frac{l \partial^3 f}{\partial l \partial c^2} \equiv 0.$$

Since $\partial^2 f/\partial c^2 < 0$, $\partial^3 f/\partial c^3$ *must* be > 0 if $l \partial^3 f/\partial l \partial c^2 \leq 0$, and it *may* be > 0 if $\partial^3 f/\partial l \partial c^2 > 0$. It seems plausible that $\partial^3 f/\partial l \partial c^2 \leq 0$. In any case, the assumption that $\partial^3 f/\partial c^3 > 0$ is sufficient but not necessary for the conclusions reached above; it is necessary merely that $Y(W)/Y(N)$ increase at a faster rate than $(\partial^2 f/\partial c_t^2)/(\partial^2 f'/\partial c_t^2)$ as c_t decreases.

incomes of W and N for various levels of discrimination by W would touch $p_0 w p_1$ at p_0 and p_1 (in Fig. 1) and would be to its right at intermediate positions.

Clearly, if inequality (A9) were satisfied, there still would be effective discrimination against N; but would it be a necessary condition even if W alone discriminates? Assume that the level of discrimination by W varies by proportionate changes in the average taste for discrimination and in the dispersion around the average. In a small neighborhood around the point p_0 the average would be of the same order of smalls as the dispersion. It is conjectured that in this neighborhood the difference between the net income of marginal and intra-marginal capital would be of a higher order of smalls. If this were true, the curve representing net incomes of W and N for various levels of discrimination by W would be tangent to $p_0 w p_1$ at p_0, and inequality (A9) would be necessary, as well as sufficient.

CHAPTER THREE

Employer Discrimination

Having discussed some general effects of discrimination in the preceding chapter, we now turn to more specific effects. In this chapter we are concerned with how employers' tastes combine with market forces to generate discrimination in the labor market. Variables receiving attention include the distribution of employers' tastes, the form of production functions, the amount of competition relative to monopoly, and the relative number of employed N. Employer discrimination is isolated by assuming no discrimination from any other source.

1. A SINGLE EMPLOYER

If one individual discriminates against another, his behavior lacks "objectivity"; in the market place, "objective" behavior is based on considerations of productivity alone. An employer discriminates by refusing to hire someone with a marginal value product greater than marginal cost; he does not discriminate by refusing to hire someone with a marginal value product less than marginal cost, as might occur in cases of discrimination by employees or customers against this person. A discriminator expresses his subjective tastes or preferences, and these tastes have been quantified by means of discrimination coefficients (DC's). When faced with the money wage rate π, an employer acts as if $\pi(1 + d)$ were the net wage rate, with d being a DC measuring the intensity of his taste for discrimination. Since d can vary continuously, the intensity of a desire to discriminate can also vary continuously. Profits forfeited are the costs or deterrents to discrimination, and they, too, vary continuously in magnitude.

Each employer compares the intensity of his tastes with the intensity of the costs and determines the action bringing the maximum net return. For example, suppose two groups, W and N, are perfect substitutes in production, and an employer has a DC of value d against N. If the market wage rate of W, π_w, is less than $\pi_n(1 + d)$, only W is hired, since the intensity of tastes is greater than that of costs; if π_w is greater than $\pi_n(1 + d)$, only N is hired, since the intensity of tastes is less than that of costs; and if π_w equals $\pi_n(1 + d)$, both W and N are hired, since the intensity of tastes equals that of costs.[1]

1. R. K. Merton realized that discrimination is not an "all-or-none" decision, and he has tried to formulate an analysis consistent with quantitative and qualitative differences in "prejudices." He uses a fourfold classification: "the unprejudiced non-discriminator," "the unprejudiced discriminator," "the prejudiced non-discriminator," and "the prejudiced discriminator" (see "Discrimination and the American Creed," in *Discrimination and the National Welfare*, ed. R. M. MacIver [New York: Harper & Bros., 1947]).

According to Merton the unprejudiced discriminator may "discriminate" even though he has no prejudice. Included in this category is "the employer, himself not an anti-Semite or Negrophobe, who refuses to hire Jewish or Negro workers because it might hurt business" (p. 125). The prejudiced non-discriminator may find it unprofitable to express his prejudice, and the prejudiced discriminator may have such intense prejudice that he will always discriminate. Finally, the unprejudiced non-discriminator may have so "little" prejudice that he will hire Jews or Negroes even if it hurts business.

This breakdown does not seem very useful and, indeed, leads to foolish statements when carried to its logical extreme. According to the formulation presented here, the unprejudiced discriminator really does not "discriminate," since he judges Negroes, Jews, and others solely by their economic productivity. The prejudiced non-discriminator simply has a mild taste for discrimination and may frequently be in situations where the costs of discriminating are greater than the psychic gains; likewise, the prejudiced discriminator has a large taste for discrimination and seldom finds the costs greater than the gains. The unprejudiced non-discriminator or "all-weather liberal" is not always a non-discriminator, for, by hiring Jews and Negroes when it is "bad for business," he discriminates *against* Gentiles and whites or *in favor of* Jews and Negroes: that is, he does not

Stated more formally, an employer tries to find the optimal combination of factors for each level of output. Classical economic theory assumes that he chooses the combination that minimizes money costs; at this point, the ratio of the marginal product of any two factors equals the ratio of their prices, assuming competitive labor markets. In this theory the money payment to a factor is identical with the net cost of hiring this factor, and therefore the minimum money cost of producing each output is identical with the minimum net cost. Discrimination does not alter the criterion of minimizing net costs, and the ratio of any two marginal products still equals the ratio of their net factor prices.[2]

However, equilibrium factor combinations would be quite different in situations of discrimination from those obtained with classical assumptions: there would be a smaller demand for factors discriminated against, and the money cost of producing each output would be greater than the minimum money cost. This is shown in Figure 2, where CC represents the relevant price line if there is no discrimination and if X units of output are produced and where XX is a production isoquant. The co-ordinates of P are the number of N and W employed, and OC is a measure of the minimum money cost of producing X. If there were discrimination against N, a line like DD would become the relevant net price line; the co-ordinates of P' would give the number of N and W employed for an output of X. Discrimination decreases the demand for N and increases the demand for W, and, since the money cost of producing X as measured by OC' is greater than OC, discrimination also increases the money cost of production. The smaller the curvature (in *given* units) of the production isoquant at point P, the farther to the left P' would be.

---

consider objectively the economic productivity of Jews and Negroes. Merton probably had in mind a continuous variation in prejudice but confused the problem with his four types of discriminators.

2. That is,

$$\frac{\mathrm{MP}_i}{\mathrm{MP}_j} = \frac{\pi_i(1 + d^i)}{\pi_j(1 + d^j)} \qquad (i, j = a, b, \ldots, n),$$

where MP_i is the marginal product of the ith factor and d^i is the DC against the ith factor.

For example, with zero curvature (if the isoquants were straight lines), P' would be on the vertical axis, and no N would be employed. Therefore, a given amount of discrimination must lead to relatively large reductions in the demand for N that have good substitutes, since the curvature of XX is a measure of the substitution between N and other factors.

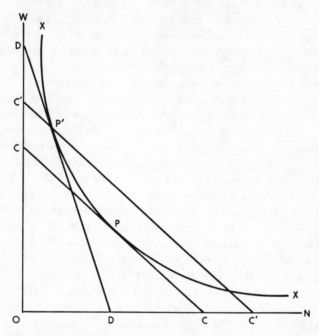

FIG. 2.—The effect of discrimination by a firm on its costs and employment

Members of the "employer class" may differ in their tastes for discrimination, and these differences can be represented by a frequency distribution of their DC's. In the remainder of this chapter we show how the distribution of DC's combines with other variables to determine market discrimination. Competition in the labor market is assumed throughout, but competition and monopoly in the product market are discussed separately.

2. COMPETITIVE INDUSTRIES

Suppose there is only one industry and a fixed supply of N and W such that the supply of N is one-third that of W. It is assumed that each unit of N is a perfect substitute in production for each unit of W; this is not much of a restriction, since the analysis of imperfect substitutes is very similar to the analysis of perfect ones. If each firm in equilibrium hired the same amount of N or W, the equilibrium MDC would equal the first-quartile DC in the distribution of DC's.[3] The proof is quite easy. Recall that the MDC in this market would equal the percentage difference between the wage rates of W and N; i.e., $\text{MDC} = (\pi_w - \pi_n)/\pi_n$. If $\text{MDC} = \bar{d}$, $\pi_n(1 + \bar{d}) = \pi_w$. Employers with DC's equal to d less than $\bar{d}$ would hire only N, since $\pi_n(1 + d) < \pi_w$; similarly, employers with DC's greater than $\bar{d}$ would hire only W. The number of N employed would be one-third the number of W employed if and only if one-fourth of the firms hired N; that is, if and only if $\bar{d}$ equaled the first-quartile DC.

Non-parametric measures of the average discrimination co-efficient and of the dispersion around the average are most useful for our purposes. The median is the most convenient measure of the average, and the interquartile range is probably the most convenient measure of dispersion. If the dispersion is zero, tastes are said to be homogeneous; as the dispersion increases, tastes become heterogeneous. In the situation just analyzed, the equilibrium MDC would increase if either the median DC or the first-quartile DC relative to the median increased. Since the relative value of the first-quartile DC is determined by the dispersion, an increase in the average or a decrease in the dispersion would increase the equilibrium MDC. The MDC equals the median when tastes are homogeneous and differs from the median when tastes are heterogeneous. Thus, while it is necessary to know the tastes of an average or "representative" employer to know the MDC, it is not sufficient, since differences among employers also affect market discrimination.

If the supply of N became equal to the supply of W and if all

3. Discrimination against W is treated as negative discrimination against N.

firms continued to hire the same amount of N or W, the equilibrium MDC would increase to the median DC. As long as tastes are not homogeneous, a larger relative supply of N must be associated with a larger MDC; if tastes are homogeneous, the MDC is independent of their relative supply. Tastes are homogeneous if no employers want to discriminate, and then, of course, the MDC equals zero.

Each firm does not usually hire the same amount of N or W. If all firms had the same linear and homogeneous production function, firms that discriminated would always have larger unit net costs than firms that did not. The smaller (in absolute value) the DC of any firm, the less would be its unit net costs. The firm with the smallest DC would produce the total output, since it could undersell all others; therefore, the equilibrium MDC would equal this firm's DC. A change in the relative supply of N would not affect the equilibrium MDC; simply, more N and less W would be employed by the same firm.

If firms did not have homogeneous production functions, unit costs would rise with output, and the firm with the smallest DC would not produce everything. If all firms were hiring the same amount of N or W, the MDC would equal the first-quartile DC, and N's marginal value productivity would equal W's. But, since N's wage rate would be less than W's, firms employing N would expand relative to firms employing W, and this would force up N's wage rate relative to W's. Hence the equilibrium MDC would be less than the first-quartile DC.

In general, firms with DC's less than the MDC are profitable and tend to expand relative to other firms. The ease with which a firm expands is determined by the relation of unit costs to output; if unit costs are independent of output, expansion is easy; if costs rise sharply with output, expansion is difficult. Firms with small DC's expand more in comparison with other firms, the less this expansion increases their costs relative to others; hence production conditions facing firms must be important determinants of the MDC.[4]

4. The only difference between a theory based on discrimination and one based on nepotism is in the effect of production conditions. It has been shown, for example, that if each firm had the same linear and homogeneous production function, the firm with the smallest taste for discrimination would produce the

It has been shown that not only the average taste for discrimination but also the dispersion around the average is an important determinant of market discrimination. Even slight differences between the wage rates of W and N induce employers with small DC's to hire primarily N. The equilibrium MDC must differ from what it would be if all potential employers had average DC's. An increase in the relative supply of N may increase the MDC against N, and this, too, is related to differences in employers' tastes.[5] If unit costs rise as a firm expands, firms that have been employing N will not employ all the additional N; some N must be employed by firms that have been employing W. These firms have larger DC's and employ N only if N's wage rate declines relative to W's, i.e., only if the MDC increases.[6]

It does not necessarily follow from this analysis that the MDC would be greater than zero. For example, if the production functions of each firm were linear and homogeneous, the MDC would equal zero if at least one employer had a zero DC. Conventional theory usually "assumes" that all employers endeavor to maximize money income. This has been continuously criticized by those who argue that some employers want power, an easy life, and other forms of non-money income. The introduction of DC's generalizes conventional theory; it is no longer assumed that all potential employers want to maximize money income. Nevertheless, under certain conditions the equilibrium MDC would equal zero, and, consequently, all surviving employers would be maximizing money income. When this occurs, conventional theory is observationally equivalent to this more general theory.

---

entire industry output. If, on the other hand, each firm had a taste for nepotism, the firm with the largest taste would produce the entire output. A taste for nepotism implies the existence of non-monetary returns from employing W, and, therefore, the firm with the largest taste would have the smallest net costs.

5. See the appendix to this chapter (pp. 50–52) for a mathematical discussion of this problem.

6. If the tastes of all employers were the same but were a function of the relative number of N, a change in the relative supply of N would change the MDC. This relationship is discussed further in subsequent chapters.

3. MONOPOLISTIC INDUSTRIES

Instead of assuming free entry and competition in production, assume that one member of the employer class is chosen at random and given a "franchise" to produce the total output and that each firm has a production function homogeneous of first degree. If the individual given the franchise had a relatively large DC, he would have larger net costs and receive a lower net income than other potential producers would. If the franchise were transferable, it would be in his interest to sell it, for he would be offered a larger net income than he could receive by keeping it. The highest bids would come from those having the smallest DC's, and the franchise would be sold to one of them; the result is identical with that obtained when assuming free entry into the industry. This analysis can easily be generalized to many kinds of productivity and market conditions, and the conclusion always is that market discrimination is exactly the same under "transferable monopolies" as under competitive conditions. Competition in the capital market reduces discrimination in transferable monopolistic industries; competition in the product market reduces it in competitive industries.[7]

The category "transferable monopolies" includes those monopolies due to patents, other kinds of salable franchises provided by the state, and the historical "accident" of being first in an industry. Market discrimination in these industries should be the same as in competitive ones.

If the "franchise" were not transferable, the assumed randomness in choosing the individual to receive the franchise would insure that the average value of his DC would equal the average DC in the employer class. Monopolies based on personal ability (Henry Ford or Bing Crosby), non-transferable state franchises and licenses, advantages from having a large amount of capital, etc., are non-transferable. As a first approximation it is plausible to assume that

7. This analysis is applicable to other problems; e.g., there is no reason why firms exploiting patents should be less efficient, progressive, etc., than competitive firms. Here, too, competition in the capital market is a substitute for competition in the product market. I am most indebted to discussions with Aaron Director and H. Gregg Lewis on this point.

the DC's of individuals associated with these monopolies were randomly chosen from the distribution of employer DC's.[8] This implies that the average DC in these monopolies would equal the average DC in the employer class.[9]

Suppose that monopolistic and competitive industries buy N and W labor in a common market and that in this market W supplies more labor than N. Employers with small DC's determine the amount of discrimination in competitive industries. On the other hand, employers with median DC's determine the average amount of discrimination in (non-transferable) monopolistic industries. The MDC results from the combined practices of all industries. Since competitive industries discriminate less, on the average, than monopolistic ones, relatively more N would be employed by the former than by the latter industries.

4. AN EMPIRICAL APPLICATION

This analysis explains the behavior of competitive and monopolistic manufacturing industries in the South in 1940. Table 2 gives the relative number of non-white males employed in competitive and manufacturing industries for each of the eight Census occupational categories.[10] "Relative number" means the number of non-whites divided by the number of whites. Column 4 shows that the

8. This assumption states that M and d are independently distributed; hence

$$r\,(M,\,d)\,=0\;,$$

where M represents the monopoly power at an individual's disposal, d his DC, and r the correlation coefficient between M and d. For my purposes, r need not be zero but only "small"; the reader will probably find this more congenial.

9. In (non-transferable) duopolistic industries, two members of the employer class would be chosen at random. This would increase the influence of persons with small DC's, and lead to less market discrimination than in "pure" monopolistic industries. As the number of potential producers increased, the amount of discrimination in these industries would approach the amount in competitive industries.

10. The monopolistic-competitive breakdown is based upon G. Warren Nutter, *The Extent of Enterprise Monopoly in the United States, 1899–1939* (Chicago: University of Chicago Press, 1951), pp. 1–169 (see appendix to this chapter, pp. 52–54, for a discussion of this classification).

relative number of non-whites was greater in competitive than in monopolistic industries for seven of the eight categories; it was less only for "other service workers."[11]

Not only the number of entries below unity[12] but also the detailed differences among these entries agree with the theory presented here. According to this theory, discrimination in competitive indus-

TABLE 2

RELATIVE NUMBERS OF NON-WHITE MALES EMPLOYED IN MANUFAC-
TURING INDUSTRIES IN 1940 IN THE SOUTH BY OCCUPATION AND
MONOPOLY-COMPETITIVE CLASSIFICATION*

Occupation (1)	Relative Number in Competitive Industries† (2)	Relative Number in Monopolistic Industries† (3)	Column 3 Divided by Column 2 (4)
Professional and semiprofessional workers....................	0.009	0.002	0.23
Officials and proprietors.........	0.008	0.001	0.13
Clerical and sales workers.......	0.024	0.009	0.40
Craftsmen.....................	0.065	0.019	0.28
Operatives....................	0.136	0.122	0.89
Protective service workers.......	0.096	0.033	0.35
Other service workers...........	1.020	1.894	1.86
Laborers......................	1.046	0.579	0.55
Occupation not reported........	0.242	0.079	0.32

* Source: U.S. Bureau of the Census, *Census of Population, 1940* (Washington, D.C.: Government Printing Office, 1943), Vol. III, Part I, Table 82 (see appendix to this chapter, pp. 52–54, for a discussion of this classification).

† "Relative number" means the number of employed non-whites divided by the number of employed whites.

11. Since proprietors are "hired" by proprietors only in a trivial sense, we should like to subtract them out of the "officials and proprietors" category. Relatively more non-white officials could have been employed in monopolistic industries only if there were at least four times as many non-white proprietors as officials. In 1950 there were about twice as many non-white proprietors as officials (see U.S. Bureau of the Census, *Census of Population, 1950* [Washington, D.C.: Government Printing Office, 1953], II, 276).

12. Suppose the null hypothesis is that the first eight numbers in column 4 were random drawings from an infinite population in which half the numbers were 1 or larger. With this hypothesis, the probability that seven or more of these numbers would be less than 1 is only 0.035; hence it would be rejected at the 0.05 level of significance.

tries increases as the relative supply of non-whites increases; the average amount of discrimination in monopolistic industries is always determined by the median DC and thus is independent of the relative supply of non-whites. If there are more non-whites than whites, there may be more discrimination in competitive than in monopolistic industries. As the relative number of non-whites in an occupation increases, the proportion employed by monopolistic industries should also increase. Non-whites were relatively most numerous among other service workers, laborers, and operatives, and the numbers in column 4 are largest for these occupations; they were least numerous among professional workers and officials and proprietors, and the numbers in column 4 are smallest for those occupations.[13] Even more impressive evidence is that the only category in which relatively more non-whites were employed in monopolistic industries is also the only category in which the supply of non-whites was greater than the supply of whites.

Since the data refer to manufacturing industries in a particular region, the assumption that both sets of industries buy labor in the same market may not be too unrealistic. The Census occupational categories give a useful classification of factors.

Even if these assumptions are accepted, the regularities in the data might be predicted by alternative theories. Employee or consumer discrimination may be larger in monopolistic industries; e.g., trade unions may be stronger there (see chap. 4). The average size of an establishment may be larger in monopolistic industries, and this, too, would lead to larger discrimination (see chap. 6, pp. 89–90). Employers in monopolistic industries may be more exposed to the public, therefore being under greater community pressure to discriminate. It is important to point out that these and similar hypotheses fail to explain the high correlation between the relative number of non-whites in an occupation and the relative amount of discrimination in monopolistic industries. However, other theories could explain this correlation. An employer's taste for discrimination might depend considerably on his "contact" with employees;

13. The rank correlation coefficient between the ranks of the numbers in column 4 and the proportion of non-white males employed in manufacturing industries is 0.90. This is significantly different from zero at the 0.01 level.

for example, he might discriminate only slightly against those he seldom saw. His greatest contact usually is with professional employees, officials, sales personnel, and foremen and craftsmen; according to this theory of "contact," he would discriminate most against them. This means that the median DC would be smallest for operatives, service workers, and laborers. Since the analysis implies that the numbers in column 4 would be closer to unity, the smaller the median, this theory of contact could explain some of the regularities in column 4. But note that it cannot explain why monopolistic industries hire relatively more non-white other service workers, and it must be supplemented by an analysis stressing the influence of changes in the relative supply of non-whites.

APPENDIX TO CHAPTER 3

1. MATHEMATICAL ANALYSIS

Assume that the supply of two perfectly substitutable factors, N and W, to the industry being considered is fixed at S_n^0 and S_w^0, respectively, and that the production function of any potential firm is identical with the production function of the industry. This function can be represented by

$$X = F(S),$$

where $S = S_n + S_w$ and X is the output of the industry.

The discussion in this chapter shows that in a perfectly competitive equilibrium,

$$P_x \frac{dF(S^0)}{dS^0} = \pi_w = \pi_n (1 + d_{\min}^n), \tag{A1}$$

where $d_{\min}^n$ is the smallest DC in the employer class, P_x is the unit price of X, and π_w and π_n are wage rates. Since equation (1) depends only on S^0, P_x, F, and $d_{\min}^n$, a change in only the *relative* supply of N and W cannot affect π_n and π_w.

Now suppose that there are some factors fixed to the firm but not fixed to the industry. For the ith employer with a DC $= d_i < (\pi_w - \pi_n)/\pi_n = $ MDC, equilibrium requires

$$P_x F_n^i = \pi_n (1 + d_i)$$

and

$$P_x F_w^i < \pi_w,$$

where F_w^i and F_n^i are the marginal products of W and N in the ith employer's firm. For the jth employer with a DC $= d_j >$ MDC, equilibrium requires

$$P_x F_w^j = \pi_w$$

and

$$P_x F_n^j < \pi_n (1 + d_j) \,.$$

If π_n declines, π_w and P_x remaining fixed, the demand for N increases for two reasons: (1) firms using N expand production, and (2) some firms switch from using W to using N. The second reason also implies that the demand for W declines, although the demand of firms continuing to employ W does not change. Clearly, the decrease in π_n increases the demand for N by more than it decreases the demand for W. Let

$$S_n = D^1 (\pi_n, \pi_w, P_x)$$

and

$$S_w = D^2 (\pi_n, \pi_w, P_x)$$

represent the market demand for N and W, respectively. From the preceding discussion, it follows that

$$\frac{\partial D^1}{\partial \pi_n} = D_n^1 < 0 \,, \qquad \frac{\partial D^1}{\partial \pi_w} = D_w^1 > 0 \,,$$

$$\frac{\partial D^2}{\partial \pi_n} = D_n^2 > 0 \,, \qquad \frac{\partial D^2}{\partial \pi_w} = D_w^2 < 0 \,, \qquad (A2)$$

$$| D_n^1 | > D_n^2 \,, \qquad | D_w^2 | > D_w^1 \,,$$

$$| D_n^1 | > D_w^1 \,, \qquad | D_w^2 | > D_n^2 \,.$$

If the supply of N and W changes, subject to the restriction that $dS_n + dS_w = 0$, one obtains (assuming $dP_x \eqcirc 0$)

$$d\pi_n = \frac{dS_n (D_w^2 + D_w^1)}{\begin{vmatrix} D_n^1 & D_w^1 \\ D_n^2 & D_w^2 \end{vmatrix}} = \frac{dS_n (D_w^2 + D_w^1)}{\Delta}$$

and

$$d\pi_w = \frac{- dS_n (D_n^2 + D_n^1)}{\Delta} \,.$$

By formula (A2), $\Delta > 0$, $D_w^2 + D_w^1 < 0$, and $D_n^1 + D_n^2 < 0$. If $dS_n > 0$, $d\pi_n < 0$, $d\pi_w > 0$, and $d[(\pi_w - \pi_n)/\pi_n] = d(\text{MDC}) > 0$. That is to say, an increase in the relative supply of N decreases N's wage rate, increases W's, and increases the market discrimination against N.

2. THE CLASSIFICATION OF INDUSTRIES INTO MONOPOLIS-
TIC AND COMPETITIVE ONES

Tables 17–23 in G. Warren Nutter's study[14] were the basis of the classification of products as monopolistic or competitive used in Table 2 (p. 48). The most important criterion of monopoly used by Nutter is the proportion of total value of output accounted for by the four leading firms.[15] This criterion obviously has many weaknesses, but there is no better empirical study of the extent of monopoly.

From Nutter's list of monopolistic products were subtracted those classified as monopolistic only because of regional concentration.[16] These monopolies were assumed to be transferable, and, for our purposes, they belong with competitive industries.

The number of whites and non-whites from different occupations employed in different manufacturing industries in the South was given in the 1940 *Census of Population*.[17] The *Census of Manufactures* gives by states the total number employed in producing each product.[18] The proportion of southern males who were employed in producing monopolistic products within each of these

14. *Op. cit.*

15. Nutter, following Wilcox, also used other less important criteria: flexibility of prices, profit rates, etc. For Wilcox's analysis see *Competition and Monopoly in American Industry* ("TNEC Monographs," No. 21 [Washington, D.C.: Government Printing Office, 1940]).

16. The products involved were brick-making, building stone, planing mills, concrete products, bread and bakery products, and ice cream.

17. U.S. Bureau of the Census, *Census of Population, 1940* (Washington, D.C.: Government Printing Office, 1943), Vol. III, Table 82.

18. U.S. Bureau of the Census, *Census of Manufactures, 1939* (Washington, D.C.: Government Printing Office, 1942), Vol. II.

TABLE 3

NUMBER EMPLOYED BY MONOPOLISTIC AND OTHER MANU-
FACTURING INDUSTRIES IN THE SOUTH, 1939*

Industry	Number Employed by Monopolistic Producers (in Thousands)	Number Employed by Industry (in Thousands)	Fraction Employed by Monopolistic Producers
Rayon and allied products........	All	....	1.00
Petroleum refining...............	All	....	1.00
Aircrafts and parts...............	All	....	1.00
Autos and auto equipment........	10.5	10.7	0.99
Railroads and miscellaneous transportation.....................	6.2	6.9	0.91
Meat products...................	23.9	30.8	0.78
Glass and glass products..........	15.0	20.3	0.74
Tobacco products................	30.8	45.1	0.68
Nonferrous metals and their products.......................	10.4	16.9	0.62
Electrical machinery equipment....	8.7	15.0	0.58
Other iron and steel products......	24.9	68.3	0.36
Other stone and clay products.....	....	40.8	0.31
Blast furnaces...................	13.9	48.9	0.28
Other chemical and allied products.	18.4	85.8	0.21
Miscellaneous wooden goods.......	9.0	43.2	0.21
Other manufacturing industries....	3.5	17.5	0.20
Rubber products.................	2.6	13.3	0.19
Miscellaneous petroleum and coal products.....................	0.8	5.7	0.15
Furniture and store fixtures.......	8.2	56.8	0.15
Other food products..............	13.9	121.7	0.11
Machinery except electrical........	4.5	44.4	0.10
Bakery products.................	4.7	50.3	0.09
Beverages.......................	3.0	34.4	0.09
Other textile mill products........	2.0	31.6	0.07
Cotton manufacturing............	17.8	325.4	0.05
Paper and allied products.........	0.8	43.9	0.02
Apparel.........................	0	....	0.00†
Footwear (except rubber)..........	0	....	0.00
Other leather products...........	0	....	0.00
Printing and publishing...........	0	....	0.00
Silk and rayon products	0	....	0.00
Woolen and worsted products......	0	....	0.00
Knit goods......................	0	....	0.00
Miscellaneous fabrics and textile products.....................	0	....	0.00
Logging.........................	0	....	0.00
Sawmills and planing.............	0	....	0.00
Structural clay products..........	0	....	0.00
Ship and boat building...........	0	....	0.00

* Source: G. Warren Nutter, *The Extent of Enterprise Monopoly in the United States, 1899–1939* (Chicago: University of Chicago Press, 1951); U.S. Bureau of the Census, *Census of Manufactures, 1939.*

† Less than 0.01.

industries in 1939 was calculated.[19] This proportion gave the estimates for 1940 of the amount of monopoly in each southern manufacturing industry that are presented in Table 3.

An industry is classified as monopolistic if 50 per cent or more of the number of workers were employed by monopolistic producers. Thus the first ten industries in Table 3 are classified as monopolistic and the rest as competitive. The entries in Table 2 were derived from this monopoly classification and the data giving the distribution of whites and non-whites by industry and occupation.

19. Although the number employed in each state is usually given, for each census product there is a residual category of "other states." Here one finds the number of establishments in each state not listed separately and the *total* number employed in these states. To obtain the number employed in each of these states, it was assumed that the same number of persons was employed in each of these establishments.

CHAPTER FOUR

Employee Discrimination

In the last chapter various aspects of employer discrimination were discussed; now we turn to an analysis of employee discrimination.[1] It is assumed that employers and consumers do not discriminate. Following the lines of discussion in earlier chapters, it can be shown that market discrimination by employees is determined by the average employee taste for discrimination and the dispersion around this average, the relative supply of N, the ease with which one factor can be substituted for another, and the extent of trade unionism in the labor market.

1. A SINGLE EMPLOYEE

Employees, like employers, may differ in their tastes for discrimination, and their tastes can also be measured by a discrimination coefficient (DC). This DC converts a unit money wage rate of π_{in} received for working with N into a unit net wage rate of $\pi_{in}(1 - d)$, where d measures the magnitude of this employee's taste for discrimination. The deterrent to discrimination or the gain from not discriminating stems from a differential between the wage rates received for working with N and W: the unit cost from discriminating can be measured by

$$c = \frac{\pi_{in} - \pi_{iw}}{\pi_{in}}.$$

---

1. An "employee" is defined as an individual selling labor or other services under contractual arrangements specifying his return by time or output.

If $c > d$, an employee chooses to work with N; if $c < d$, to work with W; and if $c = d$, he is indifferent between W and N. An increase in π_{in} relative to π_{iw} or a decrease in d increases his desire to work with N.

2. PERFECT SUBSTITUTES

Suppose that several factors of production are employed in a competitive labor market and that some of them have tastes for discrimination against N.[2] The effect of these tastes on wage rates and employment is partly determined by the ease with which one factor can be substituted for another in production. The possibilities range from factors that are perfect substitutes for N to those that are perfect complements of N in production.

Let us first examine discrimination by a factor, W, which is a perfect substitute for N. Each employer must pay a higher wage rate to a member of W if he is to work with N rather than with other W. An income-maximizing employer would never hire a mixed work force, since he would have to pay the W members of this force a larger wage rate than members of W working solely with other W. He hires only W if W's wage rate is less than N's, and only N if N's is less than W's. He is indifferent between hiring them if and only if their wage rates are equal. Both N and W can be employed (in different firms) only if each employer is indifferent between them. Therefore, if a perfect substitute for N has a taste for discrimination against N, market segregation rather than market discrimination results: a firm employs either teams of N or teams of W; W and N are not employed in the same work force.

3. MARKET SEGREGATION

Suppose Negro and white laborers and foremen are employed in a particular region. Market segregation exists if Negro (or white) laborers and foremen are employed with each other to a significant-

2. For most of the discussion in this chapter, N can be thought of as representing a group either of employees or of employers. However, to economize on space, we will write as if N represented a group of employees.

ly greater extent than would result from their random distribution. In general, if various members of different factors (such as laborers and foremen) are combined into one group by a criterion such as color or religion, one can say that market segregation of this group exists if its members are employed with each other to a significantly greater extent than would result from a random distribution of all members of each factor.

It may be worthwhile to point out explicitly certain aspects of this definition. First, note that the definition is symmetrical: market segregation of a group of individuals implies market segregation of the group composed of all other individuals. Second, segregation has been defined for a given region; segregation may occur within this region but not within a more or less inclusive one. For example, since in the United States a large fraction of Negroes live and work together in the South, Negroes (and whites) in the United States work with each other more than would result from a random distribution, and, therefore, market segregation of Negroes (and whites) exists in the United States as a whole. However, to determine whether market segregation exists in the North or the South, the proportion of Negroes in these regions must be taken as given, and the actual distribution of employment of Negroes and whites must be compared with a random distribution within each region. Third, market segregation is defined only with respect to the distribution of members of each factor; the composition of each factor is taken as given. For example, the fact that Negroes are a larger fraction of the laborers than foremen does not imply market segregation, although, from a broader viewpoint, certain kinds of discrimination and segregation may be responsible for Negroes becoming laborers rather than foremen.

Many serious errors have been committed because of a failure to recognize that market segregation and market discrimination are separate concepts referring to separate phenomena.[3] Market discrimination refers to the incomes received by different groups and ignores their distribution in employment; market segregation refers

3. Donald Dewey's analysis is marred by this mistake (see his "Negro Employment in Southern Industry," *Journal of Political Economy*, LX [August, 1952], 285); in chap. 7 I comment on his work in more detail.

to their distribution in employment and ignores their incomes. Market segregation can occur without market discrimination, as shown in the discussion of discrimination by perfect substitutes; market discrimination can occur without market segregation, as will shortly be shown; and quite often they occur together, as was demonstrated in chapter 2.

It was also shown in chapter 2 and will be further emphasized in succeeding chapters that substantial market discrimination has occurred in the United States against various groups. Quantitative evidence on the amount of market segregation is not so readily available, but crude observations of the American scene suggest that it, too, occurs on a very large scale: Negro foremen work with Negro work groups, Negro laborers work with other Negro laborers, Jewish business owners hire Jewish help, etc. Complete segregation of two groups, W and N, which are perfect substitutes in production, occurs if members of at least one of these groups wish to discriminate against members of the other. This condition is sufficient but not necessary; for segregation occurs if both groups wish to discriminate against the same group, say N, as long as the tastes of members of N against each other are less than the tastes of W against N. Some segregation of any two groups occurs if and only if the desire to discriminate against one group by members of the same group is less than the desire to discriminate against this group by members of the other group.[4] This general condition helps in understanding the observed segregation in the United States and elsewhere.[5]

4. This may occur because contact among members of the same group is more intense than contact between groups. Intense contact can be associated with little discrimination for at least three reasons: (1) discrimination may be caused by ignorance, and contact may eliminate this ignorance; (2) N and W may have different physical and social characteristics, and contact may lead N and W to value their own characteristics; (3) N may discriminate less and have more contact with each other precisely because they value their own characteristics. It has not been possible to discover any quantitative evidence that would select among these alternatives.

5. It is interesting to point out that market discrimination is caused by tastes for discrimination, while market segregation is caused by differences in tastes. Segregation does not necessarily accompany discrimination and will do so only if different groups have different tastes for discrimination.

4. COMPLEMENTS AND IMPERFECT SUBSTITUTES

Suppose that, in addition to W and N, there is a third factor used in fixed proportions with W or N and that members of this factor have the same DC's (equal to d_3) against N. It can be shown that the MDC caused by the discrimination against N of a factor used in fixed proportions with N equals the DC of this factor (d_3) multiplied by the ratio of its money return per unit of output when working with N to N's money return per unit of output[6] (a discussion of this ratio, the variable C, is postponed until chap. 6). A change in d_3 leads to a change of at least[7] proportionate magnitude in the MDC.

Members of this complementary factor may differ in their tastes for discrimination, and these differences can be summarized by a frequency distribution of DC's. If the supply of N labor is one-third that of W and if each member of the complementary factor supplies the same number of labor units, a proof similar to that used in chapter 3 shows that the equilibrium MDC would equal C_3 times the first-quartile DC. An increase in the dispersion around the average or a decrease in the average DC decreases the MDC. Once

6. Each member tries to maximize his net income; accordingly, he works only with W if $\pi_{3w} > \pi_{3n}(1 - d_3)$, and only with N if $\pi_{3n}(1 - d_3) > \pi_{3w}$. If both W and N are to be employed, neither of these conditions can hold, and in equilibrium

$$\pi_{3n}(1 - d_3) = \pi_{3w} . \tag{i}$$

Assume that m units of this factor combine with m' units of either W or N to produce one unit of output. The cost per unit of output when employing N is $m\pi_{3n} + m'\pi_n$, and when employing W it is $m\pi_{3w} + m'\pi_w$. Employers maximize money income and choose the combination of factors that minimizes money costs. Hence both W and N are employed only if these unit costs are equal; i.e.,

$$m\pi_{3n} + m'\pi_n = m\pi_{3w} + m'\pi_w . \tag{ii}$$

After substituting equation (i) in equation (ii), we get

$$\frac{\pi_w - \pi_n}{\pi_n} = \text{MDC} = \left(\frac{m\pi_{3n}}{m'\pi_n}\right) d_3 = C_3 d_3 . \tag{iii}$$

7. "At least" is added, since an increase in d_3 may increase C_3 through increasing π_{3n} and reducing π_n.

again, differences in tastes for discrimination may be an important determinant of market discrimination.

The amount of labor supplied by any individual depends on his wage rate. Assume that each individual offers more labor, the higher his net wage rate; that the supply of N labor is one-third that of W when N's wage rate equals W's; and that each member of the complementary factor supplies the same amount of labor at the same net wage rate. If the MDC equaled C_3 times the first-quartile DC, π_n would be less than π_w, and the supply of N labor would be less than one-third that of W. Moreover, since intra-marginal persons working with N receive a larger net wage rate than those working with W, they each supply more labor than the latter. Accordingly, the relative demand for N must be greater than the relative supply of N, and the equilibrium MDC must be less than C_3 times the first-quartile DC. The equilibrium MDC is smaller, the larger the supply elasticities of these different kinds of labor are. The increase in the MDC caused by an increase in the relative supply of N is determined by the average DC, the dispersion around the average, and the elasticities of supply.

It seems plausible that tastes for discrimination by imperfect substitutes would cause market discrimination in between that caused by perfect substitutes and perfect complements. To prove this, assume that in the absence of discrimination it would be optimal to employ m' units of N (or W) for each m units of this factor. If proportions were fixed, the equilibrium relative wage rates of N and W for various levels of discrimination would be given by equation (iii) (n. 6). If proportions could be varied, discrimination would cause an employer to use more than m' units of N and less than m' units of W with each m units of this factor. Discrimination causes a decline in π_n and a rise in π_w, and this encourages him to increase his demand for N relative to W; this, in turn, increases π_n relative to π_w. The proof is thus completed, because it has been shown that the equilibrium MDC with variable proportions must be less than that with fixed proportions.

Various writers have stressed the connection between the magnitude of tastes for discrimination and economic conditions. They have particularly emphasized the observation that members of one group often develop large tastes against other groups competing in the market place for the same kind of jobs.[8] Competition is greatest between groups that are perfect substitutes, and it diminishes as the degree of substitution diminishes. Thus the alleged connection between tastes and competition can be stated as follows: Other things being equal, tastes for discrimination against N are largest among factors that are the best substitutes for N. Some writers further imply that, because good substitutes have the largest tastes for discrimination, they also produce most of the market discrimination. The preceding analysis shows that this conclusion does not necessarily follow from the assumption about tastes. A given amount of discrimination by a factor causes less market discrimination against N, the more substitutable this factor is for N.[9] As the degree of substitution increases, two opposing forces operate: on the one hand, tastes increase, but, on the other, the market discrimination caused by given tastes decreases. The conclusion that market discrimination stems primarily from discrimination by good substitutes must assume that the former increases at a significantly faster rate than the latter decreases.[10] Although there is no reliable evidence available for testing this assumption, I doubt whether it is true.

8. See, for example, Saenger, *The Social Psychology of Prejudice* (New York: Harper & Bros., 1953), p. 98; Gordon Allport, *The Nature of Prejudice* (Cambridge: Addison-Wesley Press, 1955), p. 229; and R. W. Williams, *The Reduction of Intergroup Tensions* (New York: Social Science Research Council, 1947), p. 59.

9. This is necessarily true if C_i does not systematically increase as the degree of substitution increases.

10. Let S represent the degree of substitution, and d the DC of a factor. Suppose that d were proportional to S, as $d = aS$, and that the MDC caused by discrimination from a factor were proportional to d and inversely proportional to the square of S, as $MDC = bd/S^2$. Then $MDC = ab/S$, and the MDC would be *inversely* proportional to the degree of substitution. If $d = aS^3$, $MDC = abS$, and the MDC would be directly proportional to the degree of substitution. Likewise, if $d = aS^2$, the MDC would be independent of the degree of substitution.

5. TRADE UNIONS

Competition in the labor market has been assumed thus far. The analysis has several implications for discrimination in unionized markets; but, since little empirical work has been done in this area, it would be unwise to develop these implications at this time. It suffices to point out that if a union has a DC against a group of non-union N, these N may be excluded from the union; the greater the union's DC, the more likely this is. The magnitude of the union's DC is determined by the DC's of union members. If one member of the union were selected at random to be union leader and decision-maker, the union's DC would, on the average, equal the median DC in the distribution of DC's among union members (see chap. 3). At the other extreme, union decisions may be reached by majority rule, with each member having one vote and with each free to run for office. It can be shown that no platform could get more votes than one offering the median DC, and, therefore, the median would, in equilibrium, be the union's DC (see chap. 5). At both extremes, then, the expected DC equals the median DC among union members.

It was shown earlier in this chapter that, in a competitive labor market, discrimination by a group, W, against a group of perfect substitutes, N, does not cause market discrimination. If, however, a union of W discriminates against a group of substitutable non-union N by refusing to admit them to the union, this could cause market discrimination against these N. Indeed, many have claimed that union discrimination is a major cause of market discrimination. For example, F. Y. Edgeworth argued that women's wages in England were lower than those of comparable males primarily because trade unions had raised male wages and that women were excluded from these unions partly because of discrimination against them by males.[11]

11. See his "Equal Pay to Men and Women for Equal Work," *Economic Journal*, XXXII (December, 1922), 431–57. He said: "The pressure of male trade unions appears to be largely responsible for that crowding of women into a comparatively few occupations, which is universally recognized as a main factor in the depression of their wages" (p. 439) and "The exclusiveness of male

A wage differential between unionized and non-unionized labor may not arise from union discrimination (i.e., the money income of union members may be increased by a policy of exclusion) but from discrimination by other groups. A group of whites or males can have a strong union because they were the first to enter an occupation or because they are particularly militant. However, some of their economic strength might be due to their sex or color, as violence might not be permitted and political pressure might not be exerted for Negroes or females.[12] The higher incomes of males and whites would then be due partly to social and political discrimination against Negroes and females. A detailed empirical examination of these alternative explanations is necessary before the behavior of trade unions toward minority groups can be fully understood.

ADDENDUM TO CHAPTER 4

Economists have long been concerned with the economic power of unions,[13] and in the last twenty years have attempted to determine this power empirically. The principal measure used has been a ratio of the union's wage rate to one that would exist in the union's absence. Most economists would agree that union power has been imperfectly estimated, partly because this measure ignores union

trade unions has been in the past at least fostered by prejudices and conventions" (p. 440). See also M. Faucett, "Equal Pay for Equal Work," *Economic Journal*, XXVIII (March, 1918), 1–6.

12. E. F. Rathbone gave an interesting example of this when she implied that male rather than female trade unions in England obtain community support and sympathy because males usually have families to support (see her "The Remuneration of Women's Services," *Economic Journal*, XXVII [March, 1917], 55–68).

Addendum reprinted with minor changes from Gary Becker, "Union Restrictions on Entry," in *The Public Stake in Union Power*, ed. P. Bradley (Charlottesville, Va.: University Press of Virginia, 1959).

13. Throughout this addendum the word "union" refers to both trade unions and organizations which are in similar economic positions, such as the American Medical Association.

effects on non-pecuniary and future income, and partly because it has been difficult to determine wages, especially wages that would exist in the union's absence.[14] The probability of serious error would be reduced if other independent measures were also used. In this section, two measures are developed that frequently can be used either to check a relative wage estimate or to measure union power when a relative wage estimate is unavailable. Both incorporate the fact that unions affect the level of employment and the attractiveness of an occupation as well as wages. A union that raises wages attracts people to the union from other occupations, and it becomes necessary to ration entry to the union. One measure of union power is associated with the use of non-price techniques to ration entry, the other with the use of "high" initiation or entrance fees to ration entry.

These two methods of rationing entry not only produce different measures of union power, but also other important differences in admission policies. For example, there is more discrimination against minority groups and more nepotism toward relatives and friends in unions that restrict entry with non-price techniques. The degree of power being the same, unions charging high initiation fees tend to reject fewer applicants. The first section of this discussion relates union power to restrictions on entry and discusses several differences between price and non-price rationing. The second section uses the analysis of the first to understand the actual policies of a few unions.

Consider the figure, where the curves DD and SS represent, respectively, the demand for and supply of a particular factor as a function of its relative wage. In the absence of unions and monopsonists, equilibrium would occur at point P, with PQ the wage rate and OQ the quantity employed. If a union did not change the location of the demand curve it would move along DD to a point like P' with P'Q' the new wage rate and OQ' the new quantity employed. The quantity OA measures the amount that wants to be employed at the union wage rate. The quantity Q'A therefore measures the

14. A different criticism is that it may be more important for some problems to measure the effect on the quantity employed than on the income received.

gap between the quantity available and the quantity demanded. This gap can be closed in three different ways: (a) all applicants could be admitted, but the number of hours worked by the typical union member reduced; (b) some applicants could be arbitrarily excluded; or (c) the number of applicants could be reduced by "high" initiation fees. These three are discussed in turn.

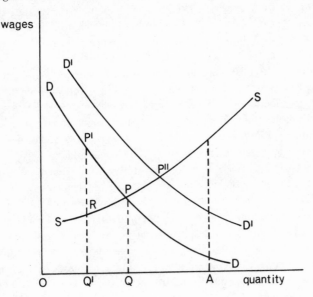

If all applicants were admitted, supply being adjusted entirely through reductions in hours worked, it might be impossible to increase the real income of a typical member. To take an extreme example, let us suppose the supply of persons to a union was infinitely elastic at the income level prevailing under competitive conditions. Then, no matter what the increase in wages, the increase in the number of union members would reduce hours sufficiently to maintain the real incomes prevailing under competitive conditions. In general, the greater the elasticity of supply of persons to a union, the more difficult it is to increase income by reducing hours. Since the long-run supply elasticity to an occupation or industry is probably very high, a reduction in hours would not be a promising way to raise the long-run incomes of union members. The available evidence appears to support this conclusion, for large declines in hours worked by trade-union members appear to occur primarily during sharp cyclical or secular declines in demand.[15] Under these conditions a reduction in hours seems like a natural way to ration the limited work available. Reductions in hours to raise long-run incomes appear to be much less common, although it must be admitted that only limited quantitative evidence is available, and I have not systematically examined what is available.[16]

If unions do not reduce long-run supply through a reduction in hours, they must do it through a reduction in numbers. A common way to reduce numbers is to reject arbitrarily some applicants. A strong union—one not faced with much competition from other labor or machinery—would reject many applicants since, over a wide range, income of the average member would be negatively related to the number in the union. There would likewise be an incentive to reduce the number over time by not replacing members who die or retire. On the other hand, a weak union—one faced with intense competition from other labor and machinery—would not reject a large number of applicants, since doing so would cause a reduction in the average member's income. Even a strong union can go too far in the rejection of applicants, for excessive rejections can stimulate the competition from non-union labor.[17] In both strong and weak unions the equilibrium number of members is

15. I. Sobel, "Collective Bargaining and Decentralization in the Rubber-Tire Industry," *Journal of Political Economy*, Vol. LXII, No. 1 (February 1954), 19–20; S. H. Slichter, *Union Policies and Industrial Management* (Washington, 1941), pp. 269–74.

16. The building, printing, and a few other unions have negotiated contracts calling for relatively short working days, but white collar workers, most of whom are non-union, have shorter working days than most union members. See S. Brandwein, "Recent Progress toward Reducing Hours of Work," *Monthly Labor Review*, Vol. 79, No. 11 (November 1956), 1263–65.

17. For one demonstration of this, see H. G. Lewis, "Competitive and Monopoly Unionism," in *The Public Stake in Union Power*, ed. Bradley, pp. 200–201.

reached when a further reduction in numbers would reduce the income of the average member.

A diagram is useful in developing some measures of union power. The ratio P'Q'/PQ (in the figure) is the usual relative wage measure of union power. It is tempting to use the ratio OQ/OQ' as a relative quantity measure of power, for along a given demand curve this quantity measure is directly related to the wage measure. The ranking of the change in quantities, however, could differ considerably from the ranking of the change in wages for unions faced with *different* demand curves.[18]

If supply were controlled through an arbitrary restriction in the number admitted, the quantity Q'A would measure the number of applicants rejected. An alternative quantity measure, therefore, is

$$\frac{OA}{OQ'} = 1 + \frac{Q'A}{OQ'},$$

which measures the number of applicants per union member. This measure equals unity for unions with no economic power, and, more important, it moves in the same direction as the wage measure. A large rise in wages may not greatly decrease the quantity actually employed, but it would (with elastic supply curves) greatly increase the quantity supplied. A large wage increase, therefore, would be associated with a large increase in the number of applicants per union member.

This quantity measure is the ratio of two quantities which in principle are observable at a given time for a given union: actual employment and the quantity seeking employment. This is not true of the relative wage measure, for it is the ratio of two prices that cannot be measured at a given time for a given union. It requires instead measurements either at different times or for different markets at a given time. Whether this is an advantage in fact as well as

18. Consider two demand curves, the curve DD and a completely inelastic one. A union faced with the inelastic curve could raise its wage rate to infinity without having any effect on the quantity employed. Therefore, the relative wage change would be greater than P'Q'/PQ, and the relative quantity change would be less than OQ/OQ'.

in principle depends on the ease of measuring the quantity seeking employment (OA).

This relative quantity measure also provides a better estimate of a union's effect on future and non-pecuniary income than does the relative wage measure. The quantity supplied to an occupation is determined by both present and future real income prospects, not by present wages alone. If a union succeeded in improving working conditions, the value of OA/OQ' would be increased, while the value of P'Q'/PQ may be unchanged. If the future income prospects in an occupation worsened, OA/OQ' would be reduced, while P'Q'/PQ might again be unchanged.

The quantity supplied is a function of the income prospects of a typical member, which may differ considerably from the income "paid" by employers. This difference is apparent in "racketeering" unions, where part of the income paid by employers is collected by the union "boss" in dues, kickbacks, and bribes. The relative wage measure would often reflect the increase in income paid by employers, while the relative quantity measure would always reflect the increase in income received by a typical member. Since the quantity measure only catches the economic power accruing to a typical member, a union can have appreciable power, yet the relative quantity measure may equal unity.[19]

A union will not move along a given demand curve if it can shift the demand curve, say to D'D' in the figure. Both employment and income could be raised without raising the value of this relative quantity measure, as illustrated by point P''. This is unlikely, however, because a union has an incentive to move along D'D' away from P''. A movement away from P'' creates a gap between the quantity of labor demanded and supplied, and thus increases the number of applicants per member. So, even if a union could shift the demand curve for its services, there would still be a positive correlation between the increase in wages and the number of applicants per member.

19. In the figure let P'Q' equal the income paid by employers, RQ' that received by a typical member, and P'R that received by the "boss." The relative quantity measure equals OQ'/OQ' = 1, although the union has raised the income paid by employers from PQ to P'Q'.

A union that restricts entry by the "arbitrary" rejection of some applicants does not necessarily select members at random. On the contrary, the union would consider any differences among applicants in choosing among them. For example, if a union did not want Negro people in the union, Negro applicants would tend to be rejected. If a union preferred sons and nephews of present or former members, they would be admitted more easily than others. Discrimination and nepotism such as this would not cost union members anything as long as the number rejected or accepted because of discrimination or nepotism was less than the number that would be accepted or rejected if new members were chosen at random. This condition is more fully realized in strong unions, since they reject more applicants than do weak unions. When a union can engage in costless discrimination and nepotism, there is every incentive for it to do so. Hence we would expect discrimination and nepotism to be more prevalent in strong unions.

A union might restrict entry not only by excluding some applicants but also by reducing their number. Suppose a union decided to admit thirty new members from a group of one hundred homogeneous applicants. It could select thirty applicants at random[20] and admit them, or it could substitute an admissions fee for this random mechanism. If the fee were too low, more than thirty persons would apply and the union would have to select at random thirty persons. If it were too high, fewer than thirty persons would apply and the union would be unable to secure the desired number. If it were set just right, exactly thirty persons would apply, and no further rationing would be necessary. Thus an admissions fee could reduce the number of applicants to the desired number. The proceeds, which presumably would be distributed to union members, represent an additional return to the union's economic power.

This equilibrium admissions fee would equal the difference between the present value of the income stream received by a union member and the present value received in the next best occupation. If it were greater, too few people would want to join the union. If it

20. Since the applicants are homogeneous, there is no opportunity to discriminate.

were less, too many people would want to join, with the result that the union could raise the fee and still admit the desired number. Therefore, this fee is an excellent index of a union's economic power, measuring future as well as present income, and implicitly estimating the income expected in comparable occupations. Union economic power would be positively correlated with the size of admissions fees, rather than with the number of applicants per member.

If a union used non-price rationing, rejected applicants might offer bribes to those administering the admissions program. Presumably, the amount offered would be directly related to the union's power. In very strong unions these bribes might be large enough to constitute a major temptation. There is less scope (or perhaps less need) for bribery in a union using price rationing, for if the fee was appropriately set, nothing would be paid sub rosa for admission. Moreover, it would be difficult to show any favoritism not sanctioned by union members, since this would be relatively easily uncovered by an audit of the books of those in charge.

A union using an admissions fee to ration entry could discriminate against minorities and show favoritism towards relatives, but it would have to pay for this privilege. Consider the union that set an admissions fee high enough to reduce the number of applicants to thirty, the desired number of new members. If the union did not want any Negro members and if some of these thirty applicants were Negro, it would be necessary to lower the fee in order to secure thirty white applicants. The difference between these two fees would measure the cost of its discrimination against Negroes.[21] The amount of discrimination "consumed" is presumably negatively related to its cost or "price." Therefore, the lower the price at which thirty white applicants could be obtained, the greater the incentive to admit Negro applicants. Since discrimination is free to unions using non-price rationing, these unions can be expected to discriminate more than other unions.[22]

21. Discrimination might take the form of charging Negro applicants higher fees as compensation for the disutility of having Negro members. The difference between these fees would then measure the cost of discrimination.

22. In the discussion of trade unions in chapter 4, I showed that even if discrimination were equally costly in unionized and non-unionized markets, there

I have implicitly assumed that the number of persons in a union is independent of admission policies, but I now show that this number varies directly with the degree of price rationing. Under non-price rationing, increased competition from other factors is the only cost of restricting entry. At the margin this cost is balanced against the gain (higher wages) from a reduction in numbers. Under price rationing, foregone admission fees are an additional cost, so that at the margin these two costs must be balanced against the gain from a reduction in numbers. If a union converted from non-price to price rationing it would thus increase the marginal cost of a reduction in numbers—approximately by the size of the admissions fee[23]—and this provides an incentive to increase its numbers. It might appear paradoxical that an increase in the entrance fee can result in more, not fewer, admissions. The appearance of a paradox probably stems from an implicit comparison of unions that ration by charging entrance fees with unions that do not ration entry at all. The actual comparison, however, is between unions that use different kinds of rationing. Once this is recognized, the result should not be surprising.

We find, then, that unions using price to ration entry systematically differ from other unions in a few major respects: (1) the present value of their monopoly power can be measured by the size of the admissions fee, while the monopoly power of other unions can be measured by the number of applicants per member; (2) bribery, discrimination, and nepotism would be less important, insofar as admissions are concerned, than in other unions; (3) the relative number rejected would be fewer than in other unions. I now examine

---

is apt to be more of it in unionized markets. This conclusion is strengthened when it is recognized that some unions can discriminate at no cost to themselves. I also showed in chapter 3 that monopolistic firms would discriminate more than competitive firms, even if discrimination were equally costly to both. The cost of discrimination might be less to monopolistic firms if they were prevented from exploiting fully their monopolistic position. This would be an additional reason why they would discriminate more than competitive firms.

23. I say "approximately" because account would be taken of the change in the admissions fee as the number admitted changed.

several unions and focus my attention on these different effects of price and non-price rationing:

a. The American Medical Association uses non-price methods to restrict entry, and the extent of the restriction is exhibited by the large number of applicants rejected from medical schools. This has been used as evidence of substantial economic power.[24] Medical schools have been accused, with some justification, I believe, of discrimination against minority groups and of favoritism towards relatives of AMA members. Perhaps this explains why doctors' sons more frequently seem to follow in their fathers' footsteps than do sons of other professional men. Bribes to secure entry to medical schools have also been reported.[25] It is impossible to determine whether the number admitted to the schools is less than it would be if price were used to ration entry.

b. The United States uses non-price rationing to restrict the entry of persons from other countries. There is no need to dwell on the large number of persons denied entry, or to spell out the implication that real incomes in the United States are considered substantially higher than elsewhere. The discrimination and nepotism in the immigration laws are apparent to all, as exemplified by the almost total exclusion of Asians and the preferential treatment given relatives of United States citizens. It seems likely that immigration restrictions would be weakened if each immigrant were required to pay a large entrance fee.

c. Licenses are required for many activities, such as the sale of liquor, the use of the air waves for radio and television, and the operation of taxicabs. Because new licenses are usually rationed by non-price methods, the economic value of a license can be measured by the relative number of applicants. If old licenses were transferable, the economic value could also be measured by the price of old licenses. Recent Congressional hearings uncovered bribery,

24. See M. Friedman and S. Kuznets, *Income from Independent Professional Practice* (New York, 1945), p. 137; and M. Friedman, "Some Comments on the Significance of Labor Unions for Economic Policy," in D. M. Wright, ed., *The Impact of the Union* (New York, 1951), p. 211.

25. See the *New York Times*, February 25, 1958, p. 1.

favoritism, and discrimination in the issuance of television licenses by the FCC. Periodic investigations by state and municipal committees disclose similar practices in the issuance of liquor and cab licenses. These practices could be predicted from a knowledge that new licenses are obtained by non-price methods.

d. If, as is generally believed, most trade unions use non-price rationing to restrict entry, their economic power could be measured by the number of applicants per member. Such evidence would indicate that craft unions have more economic power than industrial unions, since it is more difficult to enter craft unions. Direct evidence on the income of industrial and craft unionists tends to support this conclusion. Discrimination against minorities and nepotism towards relatives also appear to be greater in craft unions and greatest in the strongest craft unions. Some have excluded minorities (especially Negroes) by constitutional provision,[26] and in some entry is impossible for persons unrelated to a craftsman. "The building trades unions in St. Louis have a very definite policy of keeping the trade in the family and enforce it to such an extent that a boy has as good a chance to get into West Point as into the building trades unless his father or uncle is a building craftsman!"[27]

A trade union may raise wages but have no control over the distribution of new jobs. In a union shop contract this power is nominally controlled by employers.[28] Since a new union member may have no reasonable expectation of finding employment, easy entry would not necessarily indicate that wages have not been raised. The trade union's power would have to be measured by the number of applicants for employment per employed person. The employer, rather than the trade union, would ration entry and could discriminate and show favoritism at no cost to himself. I concluded that craft unions have more power than industrial unions because they

26. See H. Northrup, *Organized Labor and the Negro* (New York, 1944).

27. Bureau of Labor Statistics, *Apprenticeship in Building Construction* (Washington, 1929), p. 9.

28. I say "nominally" because many contracts are written as union shop contracts to comply with the Taft-Hartley Act, but are in effect closed-shop contracts.

reject more applicants and discriminate more. The possibility remains, however, that industrial unions have had the power to raise wages, but have lacked the power to ration jobs.

These four examples are very similar in spite of apparent diversity. Immigration, medicine, television stations, and trade unions appear to have little in common, and, indeed, discussions of entry into each usually emphasize unique considerations. Yet unique considerations do not seem so important, as these similarities could be predicted from the knowledge that non-price rationing is used in all four cases.

CHAPTER FIVE

Consumer and Government Discrimination

The analysis of discrimination by hired factors other than employees is exactly the same as that given for employees in the last chapter, and nothing more will be said about it here, where we are concerned with discrimination by consumers and government. Consumer discrimination is probably more important in housing than in any other market, and an analysis of this problem follows. Although an analysis of government discrimination involves several new concepts, it must be presented very briefly, since this study is concerned primarily with discrimination from private sources.

1. CONSUMER DISCRIMINATION

Although it has frequently been assumed in previous chapters that members of two groups were "perfect substitutes in production," this was not defined rigorously. When discussing employer and employee discrimination, it is best to distinguish between marketable and non-marketable output; perfect substitutes in production would mean "perfect substitutes in producing *marketable* output." A group of N might produce woolen goods as marketable output and disutility to their employers as non-marketable output. According to this definition, the latter would not be considered part of their real productivity; if it were, market discrimination could not occur in a competitive economy.[1] This distinction cannot be

1. In the discussions of "equal pay for equal work" of men and women, it was necessary to define "equal work." Edgeworth first defined it in terms of marketable output: "Equality of utility to the employer as tested by the *pecuniary value of the result*" (see his "Equal Pay to Men and Women for Equal Work," *Economic Journal*, XXXII [December, 1922], 433; my italics). He then contra-

made in separating consumer discrimination from other consumer choices, since the marketability of output depends on the whole system of consumer preferences. However, it does suggest a general procedure of dividing the attributes of any output into two classes, the attributes in one of these being relevant only when consumer discrimination exists.[2] For example, a consumer's evaluation of a retail store may be based not only on the prices, speed of service, and reliability but also on the sex, race, religion, and personality of the sales personnel; the latter class of attributes would be relevant only when a desire to discriminate exists. This example shows that any dividing line between these two classes is quite arbitrary and is determined solely by the purpose of the investigation.

Assume that all attributes have been divided into these two classes and that consumers have tastes for discrimination against members of a group, N. If P_n were the *money* price of an output produced or sold by N, a consumer would act as if $P_n(1 + d)$ were the *net* price, where d is the discrimination coefficient (DC) of this consumer. In the absence of discrimination, two groups, W and N, that are perfect substitutes in production would receive the same competitive equilibrium wage rate, but consumer discrimination against N reduces N's wage rate relative to W's. It can be shown that if all consumers have the same DC, d, and if exactly m units of N or W can produce or sell one unit of output, the MDC against N

---

dicted himself by stating that "equal pay for equal work" must occur with perfect competition (p. 438), ignoring the possibility that tastes for discrimination exist even in a perfectly competitive society. On the other hand, according to Miss Rathbone's definition, the productivity of a worker is based on his (or her) contribution to non-marketable, as well as marketable, output (see her "The Remuneration of Women's Services," *Economic Journal*, XXVII [March, 1917], 59), and therefore "equal pay for equal work" would occur in a perfectly competitive society.

2. This procedure is necessary not only when discussing discrimination against Negroes or other minorities producing or selling different products but also when discussing discrimination against the labeling or advertising of different products. The latter kind of "product differentiation" has been treated by Chamberlin and others with cross-elasticities, large-group analysis, etc. This problem might be dealt with in a simpler and more useful fashion by employing the technique of individual and market discrimination coefficients developed in this study.

equals d multiplied by the ratio of the price per unit of output to the amount paid to N per unit of output.[3]

If consumers differed in their tastes, d would equal the DC of the consumer on the margin between buying from W and N. If the supply of N labor were one-third that of W and if all consumers bought the same amount, d would equal the first-quartile DC in the distribution of DC's among consumers. If the supply of N labor became equal to that of W, d would equal the median DC. Since consumers differ in their desires, net prices, and incomes, they usually do not buy the same amount. Those buying output produced by N pay less per unit of output and therefore tend to consume more, and those with relatively large incomes also tend to consume more. Nevertheless, if consumers differ in their DC's, an increase in the relative supply of N always increases the MDC, since consumers with larger DC's must be induced to purchase from N; for the same reason, a decrease in the dispersion also increases the MDC.

2. DISCRIMINATION AND SEGREGATION IN HOUSING

a) *Residential Segregation*

The pattern of discrimination and segregation in housing in the United States has been the subject of much heated controversy. Let us assume that all dwellings in a community can be classified by their level of quality, i.e., by their location, number and size of rooms, type of construction, etc., and let us suppose that individuals or families living at each level of quality are randomly dis-

---

3. An income-maximizing employer is indifferent between W and N if his money income from hiring W equals that from hiring N; i.e., if

$$P_n - m\pi_n = P_w - m\pi_w$$

or

$$\frac{\pi_w - \pi_n}{\pi_n} = \mathrm{MDC} = \frac{P_w - P_n}{m\pi_n}. \tag{i}$$

Consumers are indifferent between the output produced by W and N if

$$P_n(1 + d) = P_w. \tag{ii}$$

Both N and W are employed only when equations (i) and (ii) hold, or

$$\mathrm{MDC} = \frac{P_n d}{m\pi_n} = C'd. \tag{iii}$$

tributed among all dwelling units at that level. There is residential segregation of a group if its members live significantly closer together than they would in this random distribution.[4] This may result from public policy, as illustrated by the Warsaw ghetto in Poland, or from private choices in the market place, illustrated by the Jewish districts of Williamsburg and Brighton Beach in Brooklyn, the Negro districts of Harlem in New York and Bronzeville in Chicago, and the Italian district along Bleecker Street in Manhattan. When residential segregation of a group results from private choices, members of this group must dislike (prefer) living near each other less (more) than members of other groups dislike (prefer) living near them. For example, Jews are segregated because they prefer living near other Jews more than Gentiles do.[5]

b) *Residential Discrimination*

Residential segregation is often confused with residential discrimination, although the latter is clearly a separate phenomenon, occurring when some people pay more than others for a dwelling of given quality. Many people strongly feel that a substantial amount of residential discrimination occurs against Negroes in the United States; yet there have been no detailed empirical studies of

4. "Ecological segregation" has been said to occur when "members of a minority group . . . [are not] distributed randomly throughout the various census tracts of a city" (see J. Jahn, C. F. Schmid, and C. Schrag, "The Measurement of Ecological Segregation," *American Sociological Review*, XII [June, 1947], 293). This definition is inadequate for our purposes, for it defines segregation in a purely physical sense, taking no account of the difference between segregation caused by income and segregation caused by tastes. If Negro and white incomes differ and if different tracts contain different qualities of housing, ecological segregation of Negroes and whites would occur even without discrimination, because income is an important variable determining the quality of housing chosen. The present analysis isolates segregation resulting from tastes for discrimination by defining residential segregation relative to the quality of housing chosen by each individual. This approach would yield lower segregation indexes than those obtained by Jahn *et al.* and used in R. Weaver's study of discrimination against Negroes in housing (see his *The Negro Ghetto* [New York: Harcourt, Brace & Co., 1948], pp. 98–99 n.).

5. This analysis of residential segregation is the same as that of market segregation in general presented in chap. 4.

this.[6] We do get the impression that in northern cities during at least the last fifteen years whites have paid less than Negroes for equivalent housing. But some of this difference was due to rent control and not to discrimination: during this period Negroes were moving to the North in very large numbers, and new residents in rent-controlled communities pay more for equivalent housing than do old residents.[7] The removal of rent control in most northern communities has therefore probably narrowed this difference. Likewise, the invalidation of restrictive covenants by the Supreme Court also lessened the difference, since these agreements had previously prevented Negroes from moving into certain areas.

Nevertheless, Negroes still (1957) appear to pay significantly more than whites for equivalent housing in cities like Chicago, where rent control and restrictive covenants have been abolished for several years. This can be interpreted as an equilibrium difference that will be maintained until public policies or individual tastes change. Another interpretation is possible: that the very rapid influx of Negroes into Chicago during the last fifteen years has led to *temporary* differences between rents paid by Negroes and whites which would be eliminated a few years after the influx ceased.

Many individuals try to avoid living near Negroes, and this is an important motivation for neighborhood restrictive covenants; but they may very well sell a house or rent an apartment to Negroes living in a different part of town or in a different community, for then it is not their willingness to live near Negroes that is relevant but rather their willingness to be responsible for others' living near Negroes. Moreover, if they balk at selling directly to Negroes, they

6. From an examination of housing data, Margaret Reid has concluded that Negroes and whites of the same "permanent" income probably spend the same amount on housing. This does not necessarily imply the absence of residential discrimination, since Negroes may have fewer rooms or otherwise inferior dwellings than whites at the same income level (her analysis will be published in a forthcoming monograph on housing). Weaver (*op. cit.*, Tables XIII, XIV, XXV, and *passim*) purports to show that Negroes pay more than whites for equivalent housing, but the data are so crude that very little can be concluded from them.

7. Even without a heavy inflow of Negroes, rent control would result in their paying higher rents if the enforcement of these controls was less strict in Negro sections.

could sell to white firms who might in turn rent or sell to Negroes. This does not imply that the unwillingness of whites to live near Negroes has no important consequences for the housing market; rather it implies that these tastes are directly relevant to residential segregation and not to discrimination.

Since Negroes are prevented from living in white neighborhoods, their population can expand only within and on the periphery of existing Negro neighborhoods. If they expand within these neighborhoods, their rents will increase relative to rents for whites, and some of them will try to move to peripheral areas. White apartment-house and homeowners may be unwilling to suffer a large monetary loss to avoid selling their property to Negroes, but an appreciable lag could elapse between the time Negroes wanted to expand and the time whites moved out of the peripheral areas: leases must expire, families must decide to live elsewhere, owners must locate prospective buyers, etc.[8] A lag would exist as long as the influx of Negroes continued, and during this lag Negroes would pay more than whites for equivalent housing. This rent differential, although caused by an adjustment lag, would appear to be a long-run equilibrium differential.[9]

8. Restrictive covenants probably increased this lag and slowed down the adjustment process. This is also Weaver's view:

"The main influence of racial covenants in the areas surrounding or close to the Black Belt is to limit artificially and *temporarily* the space and facilities in which colored Americans live. . . . Race restrictive covenants have not and cannot prevent the expansion of living space for mounting Negro populations" (*op. cit.*, p. 234). Also: "In normal times covenants are much less effective. The very areas, for example, that are now occupied by Negroes were once covenanted against them—and the covenants had not run out before Negroes entered the areas" (p. 236).

9. A similar hypothesis was put forward by Weaver when he argued that "once the concept of Black Belts gained acceptance, it was inevitable that rents would be higher in Negro neighborhoods than elsewhere [for equivalent housing] *as long as there were appreciable numbers of colored people coming into the cities* of the North" (*ibid.*, p. 36; his italics). However, in other parts of his book he appears to interpret these differences as relatively long-run differences caused by discrimination.

Part of the difference between the rents paid by Negroes and whites may be common to all incoming groups, being caused by rent control, imperfect knowl-

This hypothesis could be tested by comparing the rents in cities where the proportion of Negroes has been rapidly changing with those in cities where the proportion has been relatively constant. Discrimination against Negroes is much greater in the South than in the North (see chap. 8); yet one hears more about residential discrimination against Negroes in northern cities. This is hard to reconcile with the theory that these rent differentials are directly caused by discrimination against Negroes but is perfectly consistent with the theory discussed here, since the relative number of Negroes in southern cities has been fairly constant.[10] This theory also explains why Negro families in northern cities live with one another more than whites do. Since expanding Negro populations must occupy the dwellings in peripheral areas and since these dwellings often were constructed for higher-income whites, Negro families can afford to live in them only by doubling up. There have been numerous complaints about discrimination against Jews in housing, although the proportion of Jews in the larger cities has been relatively constant during the last two decades. It may be that a careful study of the rents paid in these cities would show relatively minor discrimination against Jews, supporting the present interpretation of the white-Negro differentials.

3. GOVERNMENT DISCRIMINATION

The importance of government discrimination has often been emphasized, and at least a brief discussion of the variables deter-

---

edge, or various lags. Discrimination forces incoming Negroes to pay higher rents than those paid by other incoming groups.

This hypothesis is concerned only with discrimination by private individuals in the market place and not with government discrimination. Government behavior may be directly discriminatory, as illustrated by housing inspection that is especially severe for buildings rented to Negroes. Or it may indirectly contribute to discrimination, as illustrated by permitting white neighborhoods in the path of an expanding Negro population to be zoned against occupancy by more than one family per house.

10. If northerners objected to physical contact with Negroes more than southerners did, discrimination against Negroes in housing might be less in the South than in the North, although discrimination against them in general was greater in the South. This hypothesis does not explain why crude segregation indexes are higher in the South (see Jahn *et al.*, *op. cit.*).

mining government behavior seems appropriate. Let us suppose that the electorate periodically chooses by majority vote one of two competing political parties. Let us assume that the only issue in the election is government policy toward two groups and that the preferences of each voter can be represented by a DC. Figure 3 represents the frequency distribution of DC's among voters. Each party promises, if elected, to act as if it had a particular DC, and each

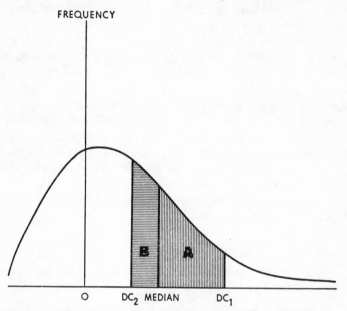

FIG. 3.—The distribution of tastes for discrimination among the electorate

individual votes for the party promising a DC closest to his own. Clearly, a promise of DC_1 (to the right of the median) could not be an equilibrium position, since a promise of any DC in region A must receive more votes; likewise, a promise of DC_2 (to the left of the median) could not be an equilibrium one, since any DC in region B must receive more votes. Therefore, the median DC is the only possible equilibrium position. This result should be expected, since a well-functioning political democracy is supposed to effect a compromise between extreme views, and the median is a natural compromise.

An application of this model to the real world is not likely to be very fruitful unless the following factors are considered: (1) the compromise is effected among the preferences of voters and not of the population at large (disfranchised groups, such as Negroes in the South and women in some countries, have no direct influence on government policy); (2) individual preferences with respect to government behavior may differ from their preferences with respect to their own private behavior; and (3) it has been assumed that each election decides only a single issue, but in most actual elections a single vote expresses a choice on many issues.

This "tie-in" of issues may be an important explanation of why minority groups often have a disproportionate influence on government policy. Let there be three classes of voters, W_1, W_2, and N, and two issues, one determining the amount of government discrimination against N. Suppose that both W_1 and W_2 consider the other issue much more important and that their views on this issue differ greatly; N considers the discrimination issue more important, and its views on the other issue are more similar to W_1's. A political candidate might not obtain a majority of all votes from W_1 alone but might from W_1 and N combined. By offering a platform with W_1's views on the other issue and N's views on discrimination, he would obtain N's votes and probably W_1's as well; even if W_1 wanted to discriminate against N, it would willingly compromise because of its greater concern over the other issue. Thus N's views on discrimination could become government policy, notwithstanding that it is a minority and that W_1 and W_2 both prefer greater discrimination against N.

This analysis implies that state governments in the South greatly discriminate against Negroes, since Negroes have been disfranchised, southern whites desire a large amount of government discrimination, and race relations is one of the most pressing issues. In northern states, on the other hand, discrimination by governments would be much less, since Negroes do vote, the desire for *government* discrimination is not so keen, and race relations is a much less important issue. This prediction seems consistent with the actual behavior toward Negroes of southern and northern governments.

CHAPTER SIX

Market Discrimination

In the last few chapters discrimination by employers, employees, consumers, and government have been discussed separately. The actual market discrimination is a summation of the market discrimination caused by each group considered separately. This chapter proves this theorem and explores some of its implications.

1. THEORY

It is assumed that all hired factors in a given market are either perfect substitutes or perfect complements (i.e., used in fixed proportions). Although the amount of market discrimination caused by imperfect substitutes is somewhere between that caused by equal tastes of perfect substitutes and complements (see chap. 4), it is sufficiently realistic for our problems to deal only with the two extremes. It is temporarily assumed that members of the same factor have the same tastes for discrimination; these tastes are directed toward a group, N, that is a perfect substitute in production for a group, W.

Discrimination by employers converts N's money wage rate, π_n, into a net wage rate of $\pi_n(1 + d_a)$, where d_a represents the DC of the employer class. Direct government discrimination against N increases the non-wage costs[1] of hiring N and raises the net wage rate to $\pi_n(1 + d_a + d_b)$, where d_b measures the costs incurred. If a union of W excludes N because of discrimination against them

---

1. For example, governments often restrict the hours and type of work done by female employees, and this adds to the cost of using them.

and if the union can impose non-wage costs on firms using N, this raises the net wage rate to $\pi_n(1 + d_a + d_b + d_c)$, where d_c measures the costs imposed by the union. The total net wage rate can be represented by $\pi_n(1 + d_1)$, where $d_1 = d_a + d_b + d_c$, and thus include the combined effects of discrimination by employers, governments, and trade unions.

It is shown in the appendix to this chapter that

$$\text{MDC} = R\bar{d} = \frac{C_n\bar{d}}{m_1\pi_n},$$

where $\bar{d}$ is an average of the DC's of employers, governments, trade unions, and all complementary factors discriminating against N; C_n equals the sum of the amount paid per unit of output to N and all complementary factors discriminating against N; and R equals C_n divided by the amount paid per unit of output to N. Thus the MDC is influenced by tastes for discrimination through the variable $\bar{d}$, but the MDC is also influenced by the variable R, largely independent of tastes, measuring the relative economic importance of N in the productive process. If tastes were given, an increase in N's relative economic importance would decrease the market discrimination against them.

2. EMPIRICAL ANALYSIS

a) *North versus South*

From a broad viewpoint, C_n refers to the payments received by N and all complementary factors working with N in the same industry. However, factors having only indirect contact with N, such as sellers of raw material, are likely to have neither the knowledge nor the inclination to discriminate against them; hence the DC's of these factors must be close to zero. Therefore, C_n would refer to payments received by a more limited set of factors, such as those contributing to an industry's value added or those contributing to value added in establishments in this industry employing N or perhaps only some of the latter.

Several different and somewhat independent processes are usually carried on in a single establishment.[2] If C_n refers to the total value added in establishments in this industry employing N, discrimination against N creates an incentive to house those processes directly using N in separate establishments, thereby isolating N from factors employed in other processes. Since these factors would not "work with" N, they would not require extra compensation, and this would reduce the cost of using N. In other words, an increase in the tastes for discrimination against N encourages establishments to shed some processes, thus preventing the MDC from increasing as much as it otherwise would. It is shown in chapter 8 that discrimination against non-whites has been much greater in the South than in the North, and, according to this analysis, southern employers should be encouraged to use smaller establishments.

Table 4 presents data for 1947 giving the average value added per establishment in nineteen industries in the North and South. Column 4 shows that in slightly more than half the industries, value added per establishment was smaller in the North. Although this is contrary to our expectations, note the following: (1) since these data give the net result of discrimination against all groups, greater discrimination against other groups in the North could offset the greater discrimination against non-whites in the South; (2) discrimination may change a firm's organization primarily through reducing the value added per firm, increasing the segregation within establishments, and so on; (3) there may be regional differences in each industry's size of establishment because of regional differences in climate and other resources: even with no discrimination, the North and the South would differ in enough other respects to have different-sized establishments.

If the regional difference in discrimination was small compared to the differences in these other variables, the regional difference in establishments would have to be taken for granted and the effect of discrimination seen in other ways. For example, since discrimination is greater in the South and more non-whites live there, costs would

2. George Stigler has recently stressed that a firm combines different and in many ways independent processes to produce its output (see his "The Division of Labor Is Limited by the Extent of the Market," *Journal of Political Economy*, LIX [June, 1951], 185–93).

TABLE 4

VALUE ADDED PER ESTABLISHMENT FOR MANUFACTURING
INDUSTRIES IN THE NORTH AND SOUTH IN 1947*

INDUSTRY	VALUE ADDED PER ESTABLISHMENT		
	North (Thousands of Dollars)	South (Thousands of Dollars)	North Divided by South
(1)	(2)	(3)	(4)
Food and kindred products...........	247	167	1.5
Tobacco manufacturing..............	224	1,616	0.1
Textile-mill products................	474	1,186	0.4
Apparel and related products.........	131	255	0.5
Lumber............................	126	67	1.9
Furniture and fixtures...............	176	192	0.9
Paper and allied products............	632	1,220	0.5
Printing and publishing..............	159	96	1.7
Chemical and allied products.........	504	630	0.8
Petroleum and coal products..........	1,242	2,170	0.6
Leather products....................	281	422	0.7
Stone, clay, and glass products........	212	157	1.4
Primary metals.....................	1,062	1,175	0.9
Fabricated metal products............	292	314	0.9
Machinery, except electrical..........	448	294	1.5
Electrical machinery.................	1,004	592	1.7
Transportation equipment............	1,703	917	1.9
Instruments and related products.....	435	166	2.6
Miscellaneous manufactured products..	154	76	2.0
All manufacturing industries.........	319	267	1.2

* Source: U.S. Bureau of the Census, *Census of Manufactures, 1947* (Washington, D.C.: Government Printing Office, 1947), Vols. II and III. Value added for each industry except tobacco manufacturing was taken from Table 6 of the summary statistics. The number of establishment in each industry (except tobacco) in the South was obtained by summing up the number for each southern state given in Table 4 of Vol. III. The number in the North was obtained by subtracting the number in the South from the number in the United States given in Table 2 of the summary statistics. The figures for tobacco manufacturing were approximated by using those from Table 3 in the section on tobacco in Vol. II.

be relatively low in industries with small establishments: employers in these industries could avoid some costs of using non-whites because the latter would be more segregated than in other industries.[3]

3. Two establishments differ in size because they differ either in scale or in number of processes. Discrimination will be less in the smaller one only if it incorporates fewer processes; in tying discrimination to size of establishment, it is implicitly assumed that small establishments, *on the average*, do incorporate fewer processes. This is also assumed by Stigler when he says: "Closely related to this is the influence of localization upon the size of plant. The individual

A relatively large amount of southern resources would be encouraged to enter industries having small establishments; the evidence in Table 4 confirms this, for the average size of establishment of all manufacturing industries was 20 per cent smaller in the South, although more than half of all manufacturing industries had smaller establishments in the North.

TABLE 5

RELATIONSHIP BETWEEN PROPORTION OF NON-WHITES
EMPLOYED AND VALUE ADDED PER ESTABLISHMENT
IN COMPETITIVE MANUFACTURING INDUSTRIES IN THE
SOUTH IN 1940*

Occupation (1)	Correlation Coefficient (2)
Professional and semiprofessional workers.....	− .50†
Officials and proprietors....................	− .14
Clerical and sales workers..................	− .10
Craftsmen and foremen.....................	− .32
Operatives...............................	− .22
Protective service workers..................	− .64‡
Other service workers..	− .48†
Laborers.................................	.00

* Source: The list of competitive industries is identical with the list used in Table 2 in chap. 3. The proportion of non-whites in each occupational category in each industry was obtained from the *Census of Population, 1940* (Washington, D.C.: Government Printing Office, 1943), Vol. III, Part I, Table 82. Value added and the number of establishments in the monopolistic industries were obtained from the *Census of Manufactures, 1947*, Vol. II; by subtracting these figures from those for the industrial category as a whole, data were obtained for the competitive industries. The analysis is rough for several reasons. The proportion of employed non-whites in 1940 has been combined with value added and establishment sizes of 1947. The data on value added in two monopolistic industries—autos and non-ferrous metals—were incomplete, and approximations had to be used.

† Significant at 0.1 level.

‡ Significant at 0.01 level.

b) Different Industries in the South

This interpretation can also be tested by examining the industrial distribution of employed non-whites within the South; relatively more should be employed in industries with small establishments, since the costs of employing non-whites should be relatively small in these industries. Table 5 presents the correlation coefficient be-

plants can specialize *in smaller ranges of products and functions* in highly specialized industries. . . . In the United States geographically concentrated industries usually have fairly *small plants* (*op. cit.*, p. 192; my italics).

tween the relative number of employed non-whites and the average size of establishment in southern competitive manufacturing industries. The correlation coefficient is negative in seven out of eight occupations, indicating that, on the whole, the relative number of employed non-whites decreased as the size of the establishment increased. Although the sign of these coefficients is quite consistent with this theory, the strength of the relationships leaves something to be desired, for only three out of eight are different from zero at the 0.1 level of significance, and only one is significant at the 0.01 level.

It has frequently been noted that textile industries in the South employ relatively few non-whites; this may seem surprising because textile industries are extremely competitive and competitive industries tend to discriminate less than others (see chap. 3). This anomaly may be explained by the very high value added per establishment in textiles—$1,186 for textiles compared to $267 for all southern competitive manufacturing industries—since industries with large establishments tend to discriminate more than others.

Along these same lines it might be argued that monopolistic industries employed relatively few non-whites (see Table 2) because the average value added per establishment in southern monopolistic manufacturing industries was some four times that in competitive industries. The relative influence of monopoly and size of establishment could be investigated by computing a multiple regression between the relative number of non-whites in a given occupation employed in each industry as a dependent variable and the percentage of an industry monopolized and the average value added per establishment in the industry as independent variables. To simplify the problem of obtaining comparable data, industries were merely classified as monopolistic or competitive; a dummy variable assigned a value of 0 to competitive and 1 to monopolistic industries. A multiple regression was computed for craftsmen and foremen; the partial correlation coefficient is −0.28 between the relative number of employed non-whites and the degree of monopoly, and −0.25 between the relative number of employed non-whites and the average size of establishment. The signs of these coefficients imply that the proportion of employed non-white craftsmen and foremen decreased both as the degree of monopoly and as the average size of establishment increased. Neither relationship is strong enough to be significant at the 0.1 level, although the degree of monopoly has a slightly stronger influence than the size of establishment.[4]

c) Retailing and Manufacturing

The effect on discrimination of size of establishment can also be seen by comparing non-white employment in manufacturing and retail trade. Retailing is generally considered to be an industry with small establishments, and this is verified by the much larger average number of workers per establishment in manufacturing than in retailing.[5] The data in Table 6 compare the relative number of non-whites in southern competitive manufacturing industries and in retailing. Column 4 shows that in each occupation relatively more non-whites were employed in retailing.[6]

d) Different Professions

This analysis also partly explains why Negroes and whites choose different occupations. It is more difficult for Negroes to acquire a

4. These correlation coefficients might be increased by using a variable giving more exact information about the degree of monopoly. The theory developed in chap. 3 also might explain these low values. The actual discrimination in any monopolistic industry may deviate substantially from the average discrimination in all monopolistic industries. These deviations appear as unexplained residuals in regressions having the degree of monopoly as an independent variable, thus reducing the correlations. This is one reason why regressions were not used in chap. 3 to compare discrimination in monopolistic and competitive industries. Finally, as n. 3 on p. 87 indicates, value added per establishment is only a rough measure of the number of processes per establishment, and a more precise measure might raise the correlations.

5. In 1939 the average number of workers per establishment was 49.2 in manufacturing and only 3.5 in retailing (see U.S. Bureau of the Census, *Census of Manufactures, 1939* [Washington, D.C.: Government Printing Office, 1942], I, 19; and U.S. Bureau of the Census, *Census of Business, Retail Trade, 1939* [Washington, D.C.: Government Printing Office, 1943], I, Part I, 57).

6. There was less discrimination by employers in retailing, partly because there were more non-white employers in retailing. However, this effect must have been small, since non-white retailers in 1939 accounted for only about 0.17 per cent of total retail sales (U.S. Bureau of the Census, *Census of Business, Retail Trade, 1939*, pp. 9 and 54).

formal education because they are poorer than whites; since engineering requires less formal schooling than medicine, dentistry, and law, one might expect relatively more Negroes to enter engineering. The data in Table 7 give the number of Negro and white engineers, dentists, doctors, and lawyers and judges in 1940 and 1950, and column 4 shows that relatively fewer Negroes were in engineering than in the other professions. A large fraction of the

TABLE 6

RELATIVE NUMBER OF NON-WHITE MALES EMPLOYED AT DIFFERENT OCCUPATIONS IN THE SOUTH IN 1940 FOR RETAILING AND MANUFACTURING*

Occupation (1)	Relative Number in Retailing† (2)	Relative Number in Competitive Manufacturing† (3)	Column 2 Divided by Column 3 (4)	Ranks (5)
Professional workers...........	0.022	0.009	2.56	3
Proprietors-officials...........	0.038	0.008	4.97	1
Clerical and sales workers......	0.031	0.024	1.32	6
Craftsmen and foremen........	0.101	0.065	1.55	5
Operatives....................	0.525	0.136	3.86	2
Protective service workers.....	0.170	0.096	1.76	4
Other service workers.........	1.191	1.020	1.17	7
Laborers.....................	1.212	1.046	1.16	8

* Source: U.S. Bureau of the Census, *Census of Population, 1940*, Vol. III, Table 2, this book.
† By "relative number" we mean the number of non-whites employed divided by the number of whites employed.

dentists, doctors, and lawyers are self-employed, while most engineers are employed by private firms.[7] This implies that engineers are employed in relatively large establishments; therefore, even if the average taste for discrimination was the same against all Negro professional men, Negro engineers would suffer more actual discrimination, and consequently there would be less incentive for Negroes to enter this profession.

7. In 1950, 88 per cent of the dentists, 67 per cent of the doctors, and 61 per cent of the lawyers and judges were self-employed, while 77 per cent of the engineers were employed by private firms (see U.S. Bureau of the Census, *Census of Population, 1950*, Vol. II, Table 159).

Although roughly the same amount of education seems to be required for dentistry, medicine, and law, relatively more Negroes are in dentistry and medicine than in law. If there are tastes for discrimination, the differences between these professions become relevant,

TABLE 7

NUMBER OF MALE NEGRO AND WHITE ENGINEERS, DENTISTS,
PHYSICIANS, AND LAWYERS AND JUDGES IN THE
UNITED STATES FOR 1940 AND 1950*

PROFESSION (1)	NUMBER OF NEGROES (2)	NUMBER OF WHITES (3)	NUMBER OF NEGROES DIVIDED BY NUMBER OF WHITES (4)
	1940 (In Thousands)		
Engineers.	0.3	254.1	0.001
Dentists.	1.5	67.8	.022
Physicians.	3.4	154.0	.022
Lawyers and judges.	1.0	174.1	0.006
	1950 (In Thousands)		
Engineers.	1.5	516.3	0.003
Dentists.	1.5	71.1	.022
Physicians	3.8	175.8	.021
Lawyers and judges.	1.4	172.7	0.008

*Source: U.S. Bureau of the Census, *Census of Population, 1940*, Vol. III, Table 82; *Census of Population, 1950*, Vol. II, Table 159; 1940 data are for all *experienced* males (except public emergency workers); 1950 data are for all *employed* males.

one of them being that lawyers must argue in white courts. Members of the court are, as it were, a complementary factor, and, if they prefer white lawyers, the demand for Negro lawyers would be curtailed.[8]

8. For a similar observation see W. E. B. DuBois, *The Philadelphia Negro* (Philadelphia: Published for the University of Pennsylvania, 1899), pp. 114–15.

e) Farming and Urban Occupations

Another interesting application of the analysis is to compare discrimination against Negroes in farming and urban occupations. For example, self-employed farmers seem to require less contact with other economic factors than do the self-employed in urban occupations, and one would therefore expect less discrimination against Negro farmers. The careful study by Joseph Willett[9] of the southern farm operator will dispel some of our ignorance about the Negro's position in agriculture and may permit a comparison with his position in urban occupations.

3. CONSUMER DISCRIMINATION

So far, this analysis has ignored consumer discrimination, although it may be quite important in some industries and occupations, e.g., retailing and the professions. It was shown in the previous chapter that consumer discrimination converts the money price, P_n, of a commodity produced by N into the net price, $P_n(1 + d_c)$, where d_c is the consumer's DC. It is shown in the appendix to this chapter that

$$\text{MDC} \approxeq R(\bar{d} + d_c),$$

where R and $\bar{d}$ have been defined in section 1.

In the discussion of housing in chapter 5 it was shown that consumer discrimination strongly affects the consumption of some individuals. This equation shows that consumer discrimination affects not only consumption but also incomes. The large-scale segregation in retailing—non-whites in retailing sell primarily to non-white consumers—suggests that consumer discrimination is an important determinant of employment in retailing. Some consumers (e.g., non-whites) may discriminate against whites, and this discourages whites from seeking employment in retailing. Likewise, some consumers may discriminate against non-whites, and this discourages non-whites from seeing employment there. The distribution of whites and non-whites between retailing and other industries

9. See his "A Comparative Analysis of the Earnings of Some White and Negro Farmers in the United States," *Journal of Farm Economics*, Vol. 38 (December 1956), pp. 1375–84.

depends both on the relative demand of consumers discriminating against non-whites and on the relative supply of non-whites.

Column 4 of Table 5 shows that relatively more non-whites were employed in retailing than in manufacturing; if net consumer discrimination was unfavorable to non-whites, it must have been more than offset by the relatively small establishments in retailing. This result is certainly of interest, but one would like to estimate more precisely the relative importance of these two forces. An extremely rough estimate can be made if it can be assumed that a typical consumer discriminates most against those with whom he has the most contact.

In general, consumers have more contact with the professional workers, the proprietors and officials, and the clerical workers in retailing than with the operatives, craftsmen, and laborers in retailing. If net consumer discrimination is greatest against non-whites in the first three occupations, the relative number of non-whites in retailing compared to manufacturing should be smallest for these occupations; if it is greatest against whites, the opposite should be true. Column 5 in Table 5 ranks the entries in column 4, the largest getting a rank of 1, the next largest 2, etc. Proprietors and officials receive a rank of 1, professionals a rank of 3, and clerical workers a rank of 6, with the average rank of these occupations being 3.33. If there were net consumer discrimination in retailing, 3.33 would be significantly different from the average rank among all occupations. Since it is not significantly different from the average even at the 0.1 level of significance,[10] the null hy-

10. The distribution of the sum of the ranks of m randomly chosen observations from a population of size N approaches normality as N and m get indefinitely large if m/N does not get too large. It has been assumed that the distribution of the sum of three ranks from a population of size eight is approximately normal. The unit normal deviate is

$$K = \left| \frac{3.33 - 4.50}{(1.25)^{1/2}} \right| = 1.04 .$$

K would be even smaller if a continuity correcting were made (see W. A. Wallis, "Statistical Inference" [notes of his lectures at the University of Chicago prepared by June H. Roberts, 1950], p. 306).

pothesis that the ranks are due to chance cannot be rejected. In other words, these data are consistent with the hypothesis that consumer discrimination does not have a *net* influence on the number of non-whites in retailing.

4. DISCRIMINATION IN SOME PROFESSIONS

An alternative interpretation of the data in Table 7 emphasizes consumer discrimination. The large number of Negroes in dentistry, medicine, and law relative to engineering could have been produced by net consumer discrimination against whites in those professions. Both interpretations of Table 7 imply that the income received by Negroes in (say) dentistry *relative* to engineering would tend to be higher than the relative income received by whites of the same training and ability. But only the interpretation based on consumer discrimination implies that Negro dentists tend to receive larger absolute incomes than do whites of the same training and ability.[11] A lack of relevant income data makes it impossible to test these interpretations further.

Several other explanations of the data in Table 7 have not been tested; e.g., it has been implicitly assumed that the difficulties Negroes have in obtaining a year of engineering or legal training relative to a year of dental or medical training are no greater than the relative difficulties whites have in obtaining this training. Otherwise, relatively more Negroes enter dentistry and medicine because it is relatively easy for them to do so. Another explanation from the supply side assumes that Negroes have a greater nonpecuniary preference for dentistry and medicine. This implies that the income received by Negroes in these professions are the same as those received by whites of the same training and ability.

Not only data giving Negro and white incomes in different occupations but also data giving the occupational distribution of other minority groups would help in choosing among these hypotheses.

11. The qualification introduced by the words "tend to" in these sentences would be unnecessary if the supply of both Negroes and whites in dentistry was a strictly increasing function of the incomes in dentistry. See the next chapter for a more general discussion of this point.

The distribution of Jews in Ohio among various professions for 1938 has been estimated, and in Table 8 this is compared with a like distribution of Negroes taken from the 1940 Census. Some evidence in this table clearly supports the hypothesis that discrimination is the prime determinant of the relative occupational distribution of Negroes (and Jews). Most striking is the fact that the relative num-

TABLE 8

RELATIVE NUMBER OF NEGROES AND JEWS
IN VARIOUS PROFESSIONS IN OHIO*

Professions	Jews Divided by Non-Jews	Negroes Divided by Whites
Physicians.............	0.088	0.018
Dentists...............	.092	.022
Lawyers...............	.130	.012
Teachers..............	.013	.016
Pharmacists...........	.109	.008
Engineers ⎱	0.021	.001
Architects ⎰		0.004
All these professions.....	0.048	0.011
In all occupations.......	0.026	0.040

* Source: The data for Negroes and whites refer to all employed males and females and were obtained from U.S. Bureau of the Census, *Census of Population, 1940: The Labor Force* (Washington, D.C.: Government Printing Office, 1943), Vol. III, Part 4, Table 13. The data for Jews and non-Jews are estimates made in 1938 by L. S. Levinger (see his "Jews in the Liberal Professions in Ohio," *Jewish Social Studies*, II [1940], 401–34).

ber of Negroes and Jews in engineering and architecture was much less than in other professions. Less noticeable but still consistent with this hypothesis is the large relative number of Negro and Jewish physicians and dentists as compared to other professions.

Some evidence supports the hypothesis that Negro and Jewish preferences also influence their occupational distribution. The most striking is that, while the relative number of Jews in these professions was about twice their relative number in Ohio, the relative number of Negroes in them was much less than their relative number in Ohio. Again, there were relatively many Jewish pharmacists and relatively few Negroes in this field. Some evidence supports both hypotheses: the relatively few Jewish teachers compared with Negro teachers can be explained by assuming either that Negroes prefer teaching more than Jews do or that white non-Jews dislike teaching Negroes (as in the South) more than they dislike teaching Jews, thus creating a demand for Negro teachers to teach Negroes. In general, the evidence in Table 8 suggests that both discrimination and other preferences are important determinants of the occupational distribution of minority groups.

5. DIFFERENCES IN TASTES

The equations developed in this chapter have assumed that members of the same factor have the same taste for discrimination; if they have different tastes, each factor would be represented by a frequency distribution of DC's. The DC's in equations (A1)–(A11) in the appendix to this chapter would then no longer represent the tastes of different factors but only the tastes of individuals on the margin (i.e., perfectly indifferent) between working with N and working with W. It has already been shown that each margin is itself determined by certain economic variables; the amount of dispersion in tastes and the relative supply of N received special emphasis. A decrease in the dispersion in all distributions or an increase in the relative supply of N shifts the set of margins toward larger DC's, thereby raising the equilibrium MDC; if members of the same factor have the same tastes (i.e., if there is zero dispersion), a change in the relative supply of N has no effect on the equilibrium MDC.

APPENDIX TO CHAPTER 6

1. Suppose K complementary factors want to discriminate against N, and m_i units of each of these factors ($i = 2, k + 1$) are used with m_1 units of N or W to produce one unit of output. The net cost of producing one unit of output with N is

$$C'_n = m_1\pi_n(1 + d_1) + m_2\pi_{2n} + m_3\pi_{3n} + \ldots m_{k+1}\pi_{k+1,\,n} + C\,;$$

and with W it is

$$C_w' = m_1 \pi_w + m_2 \pi_{2w} + m_3 \pi_{3w} + \ldots m_{k+1} \pi_{k+1,\, w} + C \;,$$

where C refers to other costs of production. With no consumer discrimination, both N and W could find employment only if $C_n' = C_w'$. This implies that

$$m_1 \pi_n \left(1 + d_1\right) + m_2 \pi_{2n} + \ldots m_{k+1} \pi_{k+1,\, n} = m_1 \pi_w + m_2 \pi_{2w}$$
$$+ \ldots m_{k+1} \pi_{k+1,\, w} \;,$$

or

$$(A1)$$

$$m_1 \left(\pi_w - \pi_n\right) = m_1 \pi_n d_1 + m_2 \left(\pi_{2n} - \pi_{2w}\right)$$
$$+ \ldots m_{k+1} \left(\pi_{k+1,\, n} - \pi_{k+1,\, w}\right) .$$

Although both substitutes and complements may have tastes for discrimination against N, tastes of perfect substitutes cause only market segregation and not discrimination (see chap. 4); hence they can be ignored in this discussion. Each complementary factor would be indifferent between working with N and W only if the disutility in working with N was exactly offset by a higher money return; i.e.,

$$\pi_{in} \left(1 - d_i\right) = \pi_{iw}$$

or

$$(i = 2, \ldots, k+1) . \quad (A2)$$

$$\pi_{in} - \pi_{iw} = d_i \pi_{in}$$

By substituting these relations in equation (A1) and then dividing both sides by $m_1 \pi_n$, one gets

$$\frac{\pi_w - \pi_n}{\pi_n} = \text{MDC} = \sum_{i=1}^{i=k+1} \frac{m_i \pi_{in} d_i}{m_1 \pi_{1n}}, \quad\quad (A3)$$

with $\pi_n \equiv \pi_{1n}$. Total money payments per unit of output to N and all factors discriminating against N equal

$$C_n = \sum_{i=1}^{i=k+1} m_i \pi_{in} \;.$$

Let $\bar{d}$ represent a weighted average of the DC's of different complementary factor, employers, trade unions, and government, with each complementary factor's DC weighted by the importance of this factor in the productive process, and with d_1 weighted by $m_1\pi_n$. That is,

$$\bar{d} = \sum_{i=1}^{i=k+1} \frac{m_i \pi_{in} d_i}{C_n}.$$

If all groups had the same DC, $\bar{d} = d_i = d$. After substituting these definitions in equation (A3), one has

$$\text{MDC} = \frac{C_n}{m_1 \pi_n} \bar{d} = R\bar{d}. \tag{A4}$$

2. Consumers are indifferent between the commodity produced (or sold) by N and W only if

$$P_n(1 + d_c) = P_w. \tag{A5}$$

Employers are indifferent between using N and W only if the difference between the unit net costs of using N or W exactly equals the difference between the unit prices. Representing unit net costs by C_n' and C_w', respectively, this condition states that

$$C_n' - C_w' = P_n - P_w. \tag{A6}$$

Substituting equation (A1) in equation (A6) and rearranging terms, one has

$$m_1(\pi_w - \pi_n) = m_1 \pi_n d_1 + m_2(\pi_{2n} - \pi_{2w}) \\ + \dots m_{k+1}(\pi_{k+1, n} - \pi_{k+1, w}) + m_{k+2}(P_w - P_n), \tag{A7}$$

with $m_{k+2} \equiv 1$.

After substituting from equations (A2) and (A5) and dividing both sides by $m_1 \pi_n$, we obtain

$$\frac{\pi_w - \pi_n}{\pi_n} = \text{MDC} = \sum_{i=1}^{i=k+1} \frac{m_i \pi_{in}}{m_1 \pi_{1n}} d_i + \frac{P_n}{m_1 \pi_{1n}} d_c. \tag{A8}$$

Using equation (A4), this becomes

$$\text{MDC} = R\bar{d} + \frac{P_n}{m_1 \pi_n} d_c. \tag{A9}$$

If $C_n (= m_1 \pi_n R)$ referred to the firm's *total* factor payment per unit of output when employing N, $P_n / m_1 \pi_n = R + d_1$, and

$$\text{MDC} = R(\bar{d} + d_c) + d_1 d_c . \tag{A10}$$

If d_1 and d_c are fairly small, $d_1 d_c$ would be of a "second order of smalls," and equation (A10) could be written as

$$\text{MDC} \approxeq R(\bar{d} + d_c) . \tag{A11}$$

For example, if $\bar{d} = d_c = d_1 = 0.2$, and if $R = 4$, then MDC = $4(0.4) + 0.04 = 1.64$. The estimate obtained by using equation (A11) is 1.60, an error of less than 3 per cent. Occasionally, equation (A11) is assumed to be a good approximation to equation (A10) and is used in place of the latter.

CHAPTER SEVEN

Discrimination against Non-Whites. I

Much evidence exists concerning the number and incomes of individuals in various groups or categories such as occupations, regions, educational levels, and the like. This chapter attempts to extract from these data information about the variation in discrimination among different categories and in tastes among different groups. The discussion of Tables 7 and 8 in chapter 6 illustrates how difficult it is to interpret data of this kind, and therefore it seems best to analyze the general problem theoretically before plunging into the evidence itself.

1. THEORY

Suppose members of two groups, W and N, that are perfect substitutes in production seek employment in either of two categories, A and B. In each category the demand for N relative to W depends on the ratio of their wage rates. With no discrimination, the relative demand for N would be infinitely elastic at a relative wage rate equal to 1; discrimination changes the location of the demand curve and may also change its slope. When employed in A and B, N and W work with various factors of production; if all members of the same factor have the same DC, the relative demand for N is still infinitely elastic, since a change in the relative supply of N does not change its relative wage rate. The level of the demand curve can be found by substituting these DC's and the economic importance of N in equation (A10) in the appendix to chapter 6. If members of the same factor have different DC's, the demand curve has a negative slope, and the absolute value of this slope is an increasing function of these differences. Two demand curves—one for category A and one for B—are shown in Figure 4. The vertical axis measures the wage rate of N relative to W in each category, and the horizontal one measures the amount of N relative to W employed in each category. Since the demand curve in B is always above that in A, discrimination is said to be uniformly greater in A.

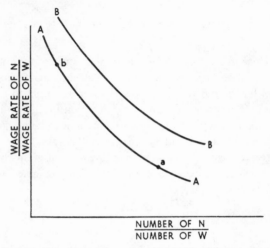

Fig. 4.—The relative demand for N in different occupations

The vertical axis in Figure 5 measures the wage rate that N or W receives in A relative to B, and the horizontal one measures the amount of N or W supplied to A relative to B. The relative supply of N and W to A is given by NN and WW, respectively. Since WW is to the right of NN, W is said to be more mobile to A than N is.

If the relative demand curve for N was the same in A and B, the wage rate and employment data for both categories could be represented by two points along a single negatively sloping curve like AA or BB. If AA represented the demand in both A and B, the points a and b might represent these data for A and B, respectively. Since a is to the right of b, N must be more mobile to A than W is; in terms of Figure 5, NN must be to the right of WW; for a is to the right of b only if N supplies a larger proportion of the labor used in A than in B, and this implies that a larger proportion of N's labor is used in A.[1] Therefore, N's relative wage rate is less in A than in B, and yet relatively more of the N group go into A. This can occur only if N is more mobile to A than W is.[2] Points a and b would be closer together if NN were closer to WW and would be coincident if NN and WW were coincident.

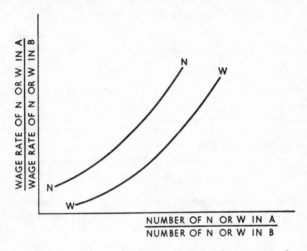

Fig. 5.—The relative supply of N and W to different occupations

If the straight line joining a and b has a positive slope, the relative demand curve for N would be lower in the category represented by the lower point on the line. A positive slope between a and b is

1. That is, $N_a/W_a > N_b/W_b$ implies $N_a/N_b > W_a/W_b$, where N_a is the amount of N in A, etc.

2. Let $\pi_n(A)$ be N's wage rate in A, $\pi_n(B)$ the wage rate in B, etc. Since

$$\frac{\pi_n(A)}{\pi_w(A)} < \frac{\pi_n(B)}{\pi_w(B)},$$

it follows that

$$\frac{\pi_n(A)}{\pi_n(B)} < \frac{\pi_w(A)}{\pi_w(B)}.$$

Nevertheless, relatively more N goes into A; this can occur only if N is more mobile to A.

implied by the assumption that N and W have the same mobility;[3] a negative slope implies that N is more mobile toward the category represented by the lower point on the line. Additional information can be extracted only by making additional assumptions; e.g., does a negative slope between a and b imply that the relative demand curve for N differs in A and B? To answer this requires information about the elasticity of demand in A and B. Likewise, the differences between the supply curves of N and W can be estimated only if there is quantitative information about the demand curves.[4]

2. DISCRIMINATION BY REGION, URBAN-RURAL RESIDENCE, AND DEGREE OF EMPLOYMENT

Data are presented in a Ph.D. dissertation by Morton Zeman on the average wage and salary income in 1939 of whites and non-whites in a variety of categories.[5] These data are presented in Table 9, with each entry showing the relative number and incomes

3. If NN and WW were coincident and if the relative demand curves for N and W were given by AA and BB, respectively, a would be to the left of and below b. It is clear from Fig. 4 that, if a were to the right of b, it would also be below b. Hence

$$\frac{\pi_n(B)}{\pi_w(B)} > \frac{\pi_n(A)}{\pi_w(A)} \qquad \text{when} \qquad \frac{N_b}{W_b} < \frac{N_a}{W_a};$$

this implies that

$$\frac{\pi_n(B)}{\pi_n(A)} > \frac{\pi_w(B)}{\pi_w(A)} \qquad \text{when} \qquad \frac{N_a}{N_b} > \frac{W_a}{W_b},$$

thus contradicting the assumption that N and W have the same mobility to A. Therefore, a could not be to the right of b, and in the same way it can be shown that a could not be above b.

4. This problem is akin to the usual one of identifying elasticities of demand and supply schedules and shifts in these schedules from a scatter diagram of prices and quantities. Both are "identification problems"; however, ours is complicated by the fact that the supply and demand schedules are determined by different relative price variables.

5. M. Zeman, "A Quantitative Analysis of White–Non-White Income Differentials in the United States in 1939" (unpublished Ph.D. dissertation, Department of Economics, University of Chicago, 1955), chap. iii.

of non-white males in a particular region, residence, and degree of employment. These entries shed light on the relative discrimination in the South and outside it, in urban and rural areas, and in temporary and more permanent jobs. Since the data are aggregative, hiding differences in age, education, occupation, etc., no attempt at a quantitative analysis is made. For a simple qualitative analysis it

TABLE 9

RATIOS OF MALE NON-WHITE TO WHITE 1939 MEAN INCOMES AND RATIOS OF NUMBER OF NON-WHITES TO NUMBER OF WHITES BY URBAN-RURAL AND REGION OF RESIDENCE AND DEGREE OF EMPLOYMENT*

| | URBAN | | | | RURAL | | | |
| | Employed 12 Months (2) | | Employed Less than 12 Months (3) | | Employed 12 Months (4) | | Employed Less than 12 Months (5) | |
REGION (1)	Ratio of Income	Ratio of Number	Ratio of Income	Ratio of Number	Ratio of Income	Ratio of Number	Ratio of Income	Ratio of Number
Northeast........	0.590	0.038	0.676	0.042	0.574	0.013	0.753	0.020
North-central.....	.576	.044	.659	.057	.625	.011	.568	.020
South...........	.411	.274	.519	.439	.369	.298	.581	.387
West...........	0.543	0.034	0.616	0.040	0.599	0.026	0.692	0.053

* Source: M. Zeman, "A Quantitative Analysis of White–Non-White Income Differentials in the United States in 1939" (unpublished Ph.D. dissertation, Department of Economics, University of Chicago, 1955), Tables 8 and 10.

suffices to examine each variable, holding all others constant. In eleven of the twelve comparisons between the South and other regions, non-whites were both worse off and more numerous in the South; if these eleven sets of points were plotted on Figure 4, the straight line joining the points in each set would slope downward. From the sign of these slopes alone, we cannot reject the hypothesis that discrimination against non-whites was the same in the South and other regions, but we can conclude that non-whites were more mobile (in the sense this term is used here) to the South than were whites.[6]

The degree-of-employment variable can be isolated by comparing the data in columns 2 and 3 and those in columns 4 and 5. In seven of the eight comparisons, non-whites were both relatively better off and more numerous in the partial-employment category. Some writers have argued that discrimination is less against persons in temporary jobs than against those in permanent ones,[7] and one interpretation of the data on the partially employed supports their argument.[8]

Urban-rural differences can be isolated by comparing the data in columns 2 and 4 and those in columns 3 and 5. If the eight sets of points were plotted on Figure 4, the slope of the straight line joining the points would be negative for five sets and positive for three. Five sets, then, are consistent with the hypothesis of equal discrimination in urban and rural areas; two sets[9] imply less urban discrimination; one set[10] implies less rural discrimination. From this analysis it is impossible to draw any general conclusion about the relative amount of discrimination in urban and rural areas.

3. DISCRIMINATION IN DIFFERENT OCCUPATIONS

Suppose K occupations contained the same proportion of mem-

6. It seems justifiable, at least in the southern, northeastern, and north-central regions, to treat non-whites as a homogeneous population, since Negroes in these regions are an extremely large fraction of the non-white population (see Zeman, *op. cit.*, chap. ii).

7. See, for example, D. Dewey, "Negro Employment in Southern Industry," *Journal of Political Economy*, LX (August, 1952), 285.

8. Individuals may be partially employed because (1) they are employed part time each week; (2) they are unemployed for some weeks after being separated from jobs known to be temporary; (3) they are unemployed for some weeks after being separated from jobs thought to be permanent. If partially employed whites and non-whites had the same average period of employment and if either (3) was unimportant or those in (3) had the same occupational and racial distribution as fully employed persons, these data would imply more discrimination against persons in permanent jobs than against persons in temporary jobs.

9. Fully employed persons in the northeastern region and partially employed persons in the north-central region.

10. Partially employed persons in the West.

bers of the class N (N may stand for all Negroes, Jews, women, etc.). If N's relative economic importance in the productive process and if the average DC of groups working with N were the same in each occupation, N's relative wage would also be the same in each occupation (see eq. [A10] in the appendix to chap. 6). Even if the proportion of N in each occupation varied greatly, N's relative wage rate would be the same in each as long as all members of each group working with N had the same DC.

The evidence on market and residential segregation referred to in previous chapters implies that members of N discriminate less against other N than members of W do. Hence *all* members of a group working with N could not have the same DC, since the N members would have smaller DC's than the W members. The N working with groups containing a relatively large number of other N can work with these N and thereby avoid the greater discrimination from W, while those N working with groups containing relatively few N must bear the discrimination from W. The N in occupations containing relatively few N probably work with other N more than the N in other occupations do. Consequently, the relative wage rate received by N would be lowest in occupations with the largest proportion of N, even if all W members of the same group had the same DC. If N does not discriminate and if some N are in each occupation, N's relative wage rate would be unity in the occupation with (relatively) fewest N, for the N in this occupation never work with W and thus completely avoid discrimination. If the W (and N) members of the same group have different tastes for discrimination, the negative correlation between the proportion of N and their relative wage rate in an occupation would increase.

There are some very crude and unreliable data giving the incomes of whites and Negroes in different occupational categories, and these data suggest a positive correlation between the proportion of Negroes and their relative income in different occupations.[11] A posi-

11. One set of data comes directly from the 1940 Census and can be found in D. Gale Johnson, "Some Effects of Region, Community Size, Color, and Occupation on Family and Individual Income," *Studies in Income and Wealth*, Vol. XV (New York: National Bureau of Economic Research, 1952), Table 8. This gives the median urban family incomes from wages and salaries in 1939 of whites and Negroes in the South by the occupational category of the household head. Since

tive correlation can be obtained from our analysis only by assuming that either the relative economic importance of N or the average DC of the W members of groups working with N is greater in occupations containing relatively few N.

4. A COMMENT ON DONALD DEWEY'S ANALYSIS
OF DISCRIMINATION

In an interesting study of employment in southern industry, Donald Dewey formulates two "laws" to explain racial patterns of employment: "(1) Negro workers seldom hold jobs which require them to give orders to White workers," and "(2) Negro and White workers do not ordinarily work side by side at the same job."[12] Since his study contains many useful insights and has been very favorably received, it is worthwhile to point out that these two laws are almost completely irrelevant for understanding market discrimination, although they may be very relevant for market segregation.[13] Negroes must work side by side with each other if they cannot work side by side with whites at the same job; hence law 2 causes market segregation but cannot cause market discrimination.[14] Negroes must supervise other Negroes if they cannot supervise whites. If the proportion of Negroes in each occupation decreases in a regular way as one moves up the occupational ladder, law 1 must likewise cause segregation and not discrimination.

---

women are heads of some households, the occupations of men and women are confounded; since they refer to total *family* wage and salary income, the wage and salary income of the household head is confounded with the income from supplementary earners in the family. Another set comes indirectly from the 1940 Census and can be found in Zeman's thesis (*op. cit.*, Appendix D). From data giving the mean wage and salary incomes of all males in each occupational category, Zeman roughly estimated the mean wage and salary incomes of Negro and white males for the North and South in each category. While all his estimates are subject to error, those of Negro incomes in categories containing relatively few Negroes are subject to particularly large errors.

12. Dewey, *op. cit.*, p. 283.

13. The following analysis is very similar to that in chap. 5 (pp. 78–80), where it was argued that the unwillingness of most white families to live near Negroes causes residential segregation rather than residential discrimination.

14. See chap. 4, p. 56.

Market discrimination against Negroes occurs because the number of Negroes in some occupations is so small that other Negroes must work with the white members of these occupations.[15] There will be few Negroes in these occupations if they have difficulty in obtaining the required education or capital, if white-controlled trade unions restrict entry, or if whites refuse to help them obtain on-the-job training.[16] These and other causes are many and varied, but none has much connection with the considerations summed up in Dewey's two laws.

15. This problem is discussed in a different context in chap. 2, pp. 22–24 and 32.

16. According to Dewey (*op. cit.*, p. 286), the necessity of obtaining on-the-job training in conjunction with law 2 makes it extremely difficult for Negroes to enter predominantly white occupations. However, it is doubtful that either law is important in preventing Negroes from obtaining on-the-job experience, for an employer wishing to train Negroes for a job can hire them as "apprentices" to white "trainers." Since apprentices are below trainers in the occupational hierarchy, discrimination against them by the latter is not caused by either law.

CHAPTER EIGHT

Discrimination against Non-Whites. II

The analysis in chapter 6 relates incomes to tastes for discrimination and other variables and thus provides an indirect method of obtaining information about tastes.[1] Relevant income data have been rather limited in quantity and quality, but fortunately Zeman has recently compiled data for whites and non-whites that are relatively well suited for this study. These data, partially reproduced in Tables 10 and 11, give the average wage and salary incomes and number of urban male whites and non-whites in 1939, by age and educational level, for the North and the South.

1. AGE AND EDUCATION

The average income of non-whites was less than that of whites in all age-education categories in the South and in all but one in the North. These income differences will be interpreted as direct consequences of discrimination, but, first, some competing ii erpretations will be discussed. If there were widespread monopsony in the labor market and if the supply curve for each monopsonist were much more inelastic for non-whites than for whites, non-whites would receive a much smaller wage rate than whites. However, it is extremely unlikely that monopsony in the labor market is sufficient-

1. Most previous attempts to learn about tastes for discrimination have been more direct, employing such techniques as questionnaires. Since many people are diffident about answering questions concerning their behavior toward others and answers to questions about discrimination are likely to differ from actual behavior, there is a need for indirect as well as direct estimates of these tastes.

ly important to produce such large differences.[2] It is also unlikely that monopsony and/or the difference between the elasticities of supply of non-whites and whites is much larger in the South and higher age-education categories than in the North and lower categories.

TABLE 10

RATIOS OF NON-WHITE TO WHITE URBAN MALE WAGE OR SALARY
INCOMES BY REGION, AGE, AND EDUCATIONAL LEVEL, 1939*

REGION AND AGE (YEARS)	YEARS OF SCHOOL COMPLETED						
	1–4	5–6	7–8	9–11	12	13–15	16 or More
North and West:							
18–19.........	0.807	0.976	0.943	0.904	1.035	0.802	†
20–21.........	.949	.767	.751	.761	0.769	.842	†
22–24.........	.721	.887	.792	.714	0.722	.885	0.582
25–29.........	.794	.855	.728	.659	0.666	.597	.681
30–34.........	.775	.762	.693	.621	0.580	.549	.563
35–44.........	.783	.718	.613	.536	0.509	.535	.460
45–54.........	.707	.681	.575	.531	0.539	.490	.424
55–64.........	.703	.685	.614	.507	0.590	.594	.448
South:							
18–19.........	.809	.688	.649	.627	0.730	.688	†
20–21.........	.905	.700	.696	.611	0.567	.608	.501
22–24.........	.902	.711	.615	.574	0.494	.575	.547
25–29.........	.817	.689	.592	.509	0.482	.461	.550
30–34.........	.707	.620	.529	.463	0.447	.401	.441
35–44.........	.650	.526	.474	.451	0.374	.363	.400
45–54.........	.565	.498	.441	.386	0.382	.459	.389
55–64.........	0.595	0.539	0.481	0.406	0.394	0.489	0.390

*Source: M. Zeman, "A Quantitative Analysis of White–Non-white Income Differentials in the United States in 1939" (unpublished Ph.D. dissertation, Department of Economics, University of Chicago, 1955), Table 15.

† Too few cases to compute meaningful non-white mean.

Another argument is that non-whites have less economic capacity than whites in the same age-education category. One variant of this argument stresses the difference in "quality" of education received by whites and non-whites, so that non-whites with the same years

2. This assertion is supported by the results in the study by R. Bunting, *Employer Concentration in Local Labor Markets* (Chapel Hill: University of North Carolina Press, 1962).

of schooling as whites have less capital invested in them through education and thus have less economic capacity. Capital invested through schooling surely accounts for a larger fraction of the income of those with much schooling than of those with little schooling; therefore, any difference in quality of schooling between whites and non-whites would show up more in the former than in the latter, unless the relative quality of non-white schooling increased from

TABLE 11

NEGROES AS A PER CENT OF NATIVE WHITE URBAN MALE
WAGE OR SALARY WORKERS BY AGE, EDUCA-
TION, AND REGION*

REGION AND AGE (YEARS)	YEARS OF SCHOOL COMPLETED							
	1–4	5–6	7–8	9–11	12	13–15	16 or More	Total
North and West:								
18–19..	17.81	16.52	5.33	3.84	1.73	0.79	4.76†	3.40
20–21..	33.65	14.13	4.86	4.24	1.79	1.30	0.35	3.28
22–24..	36.65	19.52	5.02	4.33	1.82	1.81	0.41	3.45
25–29..	51.48	20.32	5.26	4.35	2.35	2.36	1.09	4.27
30–34..	49.41	25.32	5.86	3.90	2.36	2.59	1.31	5.11
35–44..	57.09	23.22	6.10	4.10	2.76	3.19	1.93	6.78
45–54..	36.04	15.21	4.74	3.52	2.77	2.80	2.26	6.41
55–64..	22.38	10.26	3.67	2.67	1.84	3.07	2.12	5.31
Total.	38.92	18.23	5.26	4.02	2.24	2.47	1.50	5.22
South:								
18–19..	147.85	97.89	43.74	23.58	7.46	7.17	....	34.22
20–21..	166.82	105.74	46.01	21.60	9.06	6.59	5.19	30.43
22–24..	197.76	103.71	41.36	19.67	9.10	7.59	5.57	29.41
25–29..	196.63	111.43	39.43	18.33	8.88	6.85	7.30	31.46
30–34..	204.20	97.87	32.08	16.37	7.53	6.66	7.62	32.71
35–44..	197.26	88.31	26.72	12.83	7.30	7.22	7.49	36.46
45–54..	118.10	47.26	15.28	9.68	5.58	4.79	7.94	26.28
55–64..	161.28	64.46	23.61	20.26	9.87	13.22	14.19	43.56
Total.	171.82	83.37	29.17	16.70	8.06	7.05	7.73	32.82

* Source: Zeman, *op. cit.*, Table 15.
† Very few persons in this class.

lower to higher schooling categories.[3] Therefore, this hypothesis implies that if whites in various age-education categories have the same incomes, non-whites in the lower education categories have larger incomes than non-whites in the higher ones. The quality of non-white education may be lower than that of whites in some respects, but these data contradict the view that differences in quality of education greatly reduce non-white incomes. Zeman computed a regression of non-white on white income for all age-education categories in each region and found that white income almost completely determined non-white income: if whites in two age-education categories received about the same income, non-whites in these categories also did.[4]

Within an educational category, incomes of both whites and non-whites increase with age, and this can be attributed in the main to the increasing experience acquired with age. The difference between white and non-white incomes within an age-education category could result from a difference in experience (that is independent of market discrimination) if the "quality" of non-market experience was substantially lower for non-whites than for whites. However, the same kind of argument which proved that these income differentials were not caused mainly by a difference in quality of education also proves that they were not caused mainly by a difference in quality of experience.

The observed differentials may have resulted from the combined effects of differences in quality of experience and education. In the South, whites of twenty-two to twenty-four years of age and with nine to eleven years of schooling have about the same income as whites of fifty-five to sixty-four years of age and with one to four

3. However, non-white inferiority in quality seems more noticeable at the college and high-school levels than at the grammar-school level.

4. M. Zeman, "A Quantitative Analysis of White–Non-white Income Differentials in the United States in 1939" (unpublished Ph.D. dissertation, Department of Economics, University of Chicago, 1955), chap. iv. The correlation coefficients are of the order of 0.98, and the age-education points deviate very little from the regression lines (see his Figs. 1 and 2).

years of schooling. Therefore, if non-whites of twenty-two to twenty-four years of age and with nine to eleven years of schooling had lower incomes than non-whites of fifty-five to sixty-four years of age and with one to four years of schooling because of differences in quality of schooling, they would have higher incomes because of differences in quality of experience. In general, then, non-whites have the same income whenever whites have the same income if these quality differences exactly offset each other. It seems unlikely that this is the case; if it is not and if these differences are important, there should be a much weaker connection between white and non-white incomes. For this and other reasons it seems improbable that quality differences are the major determinant of these income differentials, although they may be a minor one.

Other variants of the argument that non-whites have less capacity than whites are based on differences in innate capacities, ambition, tastes for leisure, etc. In view of the limited evidence available, it is difficult either to accept or completely to reject these alternatives. They may explain part of these income differentials, but it seems probable that discrimination is, either directly or indirectly, the major explanation, and this will be assumed in the remainder of this chapter.

Therefore, whites and non-whites in the same age-education category are assumed to be perfect substitutes in production. In each category there are supply and demand schedules for whites and non-whites, and the interaction of these schedules produces the observations in Tables 10 and 11 (see chap. 7). Information about the relative amounts of discrimination in different categories and regions was obtained by computing for each region a regression of the relative supply of non-whites on their relative income. They are of this form:

$$\log \frac{N(ij)}{W(ij)} = a + b \log \frac{\pi_n(ij)}{\pi_w(ij)} + u,$$

where $N(ij)$ is the number of non-whites in the ith age and jth education category; $\pi_n(ij)$ is the non-white wage and salary income in the same category; u is a random variable; etc. This equation depends on the parameters a and b, where b is the elasticity of $N(ij)/W(ij)$ with respect to $\pi_n(ij)/\pi_w(ij)$. The estimates are[5]

$$\left.\begin{array}{l} \hat{a}_n = 1.75 \\ \hat{b}_n = 0.086 \end{array}\right\} \text{ for the North,}$$

and

$$\left.\begin{array}{l} \hat{a}_s = 1.52 \\ \hat{b}_s = 0.146 \end{array}\right\} \text{ for the South.}$$

5. The correlation coefficients are 0.53 and 0.76 for the North and South, respectively, and both are significantly different from zero at the 0.001 level of significance; moreover, $\hat{b}_n$ is not significantly different from $\hat{b}_s$ at the 0.02 level.

Persons eighteen to nineteen years old are just entering the permanent labor force; at this age, knowledge of the labor market is relatively meager, and aptitudes and desires not too well known. Since behavior in this age group is greatly affected by temporary and random forces, it is desirable to attach less importance to these data. There are also special reasons for this: (1) No data are available for persons with sixteen or more years of schooling, and this category would have to receive a zero weight. (2) Whites and non-whites with thirteen to fifteen years of schooling have a smaller average income than some eighteen- to nineteen-year-olds with less schooling. This is evidence that the income of the former comes partly from part-time work, and a bias would result if non-whites in college worked more hours than whites in college do. (3) In the North, non-whites with twelve years of schooling have larger incomes than whites, and this seems implausible; it is also difficult to use this observation in some of the statistical analysis discussed later. For these reasons it was decided to omit all the data for persons eighteen to nineteen years old. Persons of twenty to twenty-one years with sixteen or more years of schooling are omitted in the North for lack of data and in the South to maintain comparability of the regressions for the two regions.

For a partial check of the analysis, regressions were computed for as many points as possible, using all categories except persons eighteen to twenty-one years old with sixteen or more years of schooling. The following estimates were obtained:

$$\left.\begin{array}{l} \hat{a}_n = 1.78 \\ \hat{b}_n = 0.074 \\ r_n = 0.41 \end{array}\right\} \text{ for the North,}$$

and

$$\left.\begin{array}{l} \hat{a}_s = 1.54 \\ \hat{b}_s = 0.137 \\ r_s = 0.70 \end{array}\right\} \text{ for the South.}$$

Both r_n and r_s are significantly different from zero, and $\hat{b}_n$ is not significantly different from $\hat{b}_s$ at the 0.03 level.

Since the elasticities are positive and since relatively more non-whites are in the lower education categories, discrimination must be greater in the higher ones (see chap. 7). The elasticity b and the intercept a result from the interaction of supply and demand functions in each category. The parameters in these functions specify the relative supply and demand for whites and non-whites in each category and the elasticities of supply and demand. Our knowledge of these parameters is too meager to help in interpreting the observed values of a and b, but the approximate equality of $\hat{b}_n$ and $\hat{b}_s$ does suggest that relative demands, relative supplies, and elasticities are about the same in the South and in the North. The difference between $\hat{a}_n$ and $\hat{a}_s$ can be explained by the difference either in the level of demand or in the relative number of non-whites in the two regions.

2. REGION

Let us explore this further. Table 10 and the difference between $\hat{a}_s$ and $\hat{a}_n$ show that the ratio of non-white to white income is smaller in the South for almost all age-education categories. This will not surprise most readers, as it has long been recognized that non-whites are economically worse off in the South. Yet the reasons for this have not been carefully investigated, as it has usually been assumed, without much elaboration, that southerners are more prejudiced against non-whites. Several variables in addition to tastes have been shown to affect market discrimination; they can be divided into two categories—those operating through tastes and those operating in conjunction with tastes. In the next few pages an attempt is made to determine which variables were more important in creating this regional difference in market discrimination.

Chapters 3, 4, and 5 show that the greater the extent of monopoly, trade unionism, and government discrimination, the greater the market discrimination against a minority. There is more state government intervention against non-whites in the South, but more trade unionism and (perhaps) monopoly in the North. Trade unions and monopolies have probably had relatively little influence on incomes;[6] it is not possible to compare this influence with that of state (and federal) governments, since the latter has never been systematically discussed.

There is no systematic tendency for the average size of establishment in each industry to differ between the North and the South (see pp. 86–87). If the establishment is the basic productive unit, this suggests that in the absence of discrimination the relative importance of each occupational group in the productive process would not differ greatly between regions. Therefore, a regional difference in the variable R (see the equations of chap. 6) would result from, rather than cause, a regional difference in discrimination.

If members of the same factor have different tastes for discrimination, an increase in the relative supply of non-whites increases the equilibrium market discrimination against them, even if all tastes remain fixed (see chaps. 3–6).

Many investigators have asserted that a change in the relative supply of a group changes the equilibrium market discrimination, not because relative supply determines market discrimination in *conjunction* with tastes and other variables but because it partly determines tastes themselves.[7] They seem to believe that, because market discrimination against minorities is usually greatest in areas with relatively large numbers of them, prejudice (i.e., tastes for discrimination) must be an increasing function of their relative supply. This is an erroneous belief: it has been emphasized throughout this book that a change in their relative supply can change market dis-

6. See G. W. Nutter, *The Extent of Enterprise Monopoly in the United States, 1899–1939* (Chicago: University of Chicago Press, 1951); George Stigler, *Five Lectures on Economic Problems* (London: Longmans, Green & Co., 1949), lecture 5; A. C. Harberger, "Monopoly and Resource Misallocation," *Proceedings of the American Economic Review*, XLIV (May, 1954), 77–92; and M. Friedman, "Some Comments on the Significance of Labor Unions for Economic Policy," in *The Impact of the Union*, ed. D. M. Wright (New York: Harcourt, Brace & Co., 1951), pp. 204–34.

7. See, for example, Gordon Allport, *The Nature of Prejudice* (Cambridge, Mass.: Addison-Wesley Press, 1955), p. 227; Williams, *The Reduction of Intergroup Tensions* (New York: Social Science Research Council, 1947), p. 57; Saenger, *The Social Psychology of Prejudice* (New York: Harper & Bros., 1953), p. 99; and *Business Week*, December 18, 1954, p. 9.

crimination even though tastes do not change. Nevertheless, relative supply may affect tastes, and it seems worthwhile to try to estimate this effect empirically. Many other variables may also affect tastes, but it is not possible to discuss them separately.

Let us first try to determine whether the regional difference in market discrimination was caused by a regional difference in the relative supply of non-whites acting in conjunction with tastes. It would be easy to isolate this effect if the relative demand curves for non-whites in each region were the same in all age-education categories, for then differences in market discrimination between categories in the same region would result from differences in the proportion of non-whites in these categories. Since it is known from an earlier analysis in this chapter that the relative demand curve differed quite substantially between categories, a more indirect approach must be developed. It is assumed that any regional difference in taste must be uniform for all categories; in other words, regional tastes can differ only by a scale factor. Thus if in each region the proportion of non-whites in two categories is the same and if in the South the equilibrium MDC is k times as large in one category as in the other it must also be k times as large in the North. The regressions computed earlier in this chapter support this assumption; the regression for the South differed essentially only in height from that for the North. The regressions of non-white income on white income also differed only in height.[8]

If MDC (ij, r) is the MDC in the ith age and jth education category in the rth region ($r = n$ [North] or s [South]), define

$$Y(ij) = \frac{\text{MDC}(ij, s)}{\text{MDC}(ij, n)}.$$

If $N/T(ij, r)$ is the ratio of the number of non-whites to the total number in the ijth class in the rth region, define

$$X(ij) = \frac{N/T(ij, s)}{N/T(ij, n)}.$$

If there was no regional difference in tastes and if market discrimination depended largely on the proportion of non-whites in a category,

8. Zeman, *op. cit.*, Figs. 1 and 2.

$Y(ij)$ would increase as $X(ij)$ increased, and $Y(ij)$ would equal 1 when $X(ij)$ equaled 1; there would be a function $Y = F(x)$, with $F'(x) > 0$, and $F(1) = 1$. On the other hand, if the regional differences in tastes was quite large and the population of non-whites had no effect on market discrimination, Y would be independent of X and completely dependent on this regional taste difference; there would be a zero correlation coefficient between Y and X as $Y = F(x) \equiv C > 1$. In the intermediate cases the regional difference in tastes and proportions are both significant; $F'(x) > 0$ and $F(1) > 1$.[9]

It is not possible to choose among these models simply from a priori or casual considerations, but the data in Tables 10 and 11 make it possible to obtain some quantitative evidence of their relative merits. A series of observations on X and Y were computed from these data, and, by the least-squares method, a linear function of the form $F = a + bX$ was fitted to these observations. The estimates obtained are $\hat{a} = 2.01$, $\hat{b} = -0.02$, and $r = -0.06$, where r is the correlation coefficient.[10] Both $\hat{b}$ and r are very small and not significantly different from zero; indeed, if the true correlation coefficient were really zero, r would be at least as large as $|0.06|$ more than six out of every ten times. The small and insignificant estimates of b and r imply that the proportion of non-whites in a category had little effect on market discrimination. Presumably, $\hat{b}$ was

9. It has been assumed that Y depends only on X and not on $N/T(ij, n)$ or $N/T(ij, s)$ separately. This formulation would be entirely justified if the relative demand curve in each category had a constant elasticity.

10. The same categories were omitted and the same weighting system was used as in the regressions computed earlier in the chapter (see p. 115). A regression from all the available data gives $\hat{a} = 2.28$, $\hat{b} = 0.03$, and $r = 0.02$.

There is the usual problem of fitting an appropriate functional form to the data. If the relative demand curves were of constant elasticity, an argument could be made for taking the regression of log Y on log X, i.e., for fitting a function of the form

$$\log Y = a' + b' \log X .$$

The estimates are $\hat{a}' = 0.19$, $\hat{b}' = 0.10$, and $r = 0.10$. The value of r is slightly higher than that obtained with a simple linear function, but $\hat{b}'$ and r are still not significant, even at the 0.4 level. A regression from all the data gives $\hat{a}' = 0.16$, $\hat{b}' = 0.23$, and $r = 0.17$. The estimates of b' and r have been raised further but are still not significant at the 0.2 level.

negative because a negative effect due to random forces was greater than any positive effect due to proportions.[11] If proportions had no effect, the regional difference in market discrimination would have been caused entirely by a regional difference in tastes. The latter could be estimated by fitting a function of the form $Y = c$ to the

11. This interpretation is supported by the fact that all other estimates of b have been positive: in n. 9, b was estimated as $+0.03$, and b' as $+0.1$ and $+0.23$. The negative value was caused by only one point (marked by a Δ in Fig. 6), and the estimate of b would be $+0.03$ if this point were omitted.

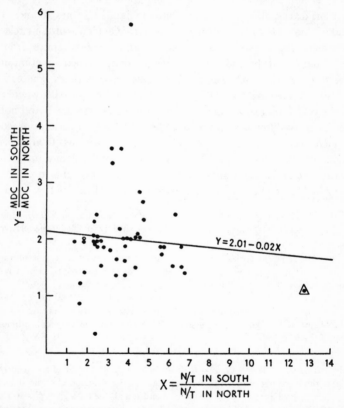

Fig. 6.—A scatter diagram of the relative market discrimination and relative number of non-white males in different age-education classes in 1939.

various observations of Y. By the method of least squares, c was estimated to be 1.91.[12]

One conclusion from this analysis is that the proportion of non-whites in an age-education category had little effect on the market discrimination in that category; in other words, the relative demand for non-whites was very elastic in each category. Within each region, members of the same factor must have differed only slightly in their tastes for discrimination.[13] Since the regional difference in market discrimination is not explained by the regional distribution of non-whites, it must be "explained" by a regional difference in tastes. Individuals in the South appear to have had, on the average, slightly less than twice as much taste for discrimination as those in the North.[14]

12. The standard error of this estimate is 0.12. It is known with 95 per cent confidence that c fell within the interval 1.91 ± 0.24. The discussion in the text has been confined to linear functions; important deviations from linearity often produce a large standard error relative to the estimate of c. Since 1.91 is about sixteen times 0.12, linear functions seem to fit the data as well as non-linear ones. This should also be clear from the scatter in Fig. 6. If all available data were used, c would be estimated at 2.40.

13. Appreciable errors may have occurred in measuring the income and number of whites and non-whites in different categories. Since X and Y are complicated quotients of the income and number data, they probably contain even greater measurement errors. Random errors of measurement in Y reduce the correlation coefficient but do not bias the estimate of the slope b (and the elasticity b'), while random errors in X both reduce the correlation coefficient and bias the estimates of b (and b') downward. Therefore, the effect of proportions on market discrimination is systematically underestimated, and this underestimate is the more serious, the greater the errors in X. It is not possible to estimate the extent of bias in b and b' until some reasonable estimate can be made of the error in X.

14. It was shown in chap. 6 (eq. [A11]) that the MDC against any group is approximated by

$$\text{MDC} \approxeq R\,(\bar{d} + d_c) \equiv 2Rd \,,$$

where d is an average taste for discrimination of all factors, employers, and consumers working with or buying from this group. If R is the same for two groups, the ratio of the MDC against these groups equals the ratio of the average taste

It was concluded in chapter 3 that southern employers in competitive industries discriminated much less than those in monopolistic ones, and this is not necessarily inconsistent with the conclusion that the regional difference in the proportion of non-whites did not directly cause the regional difference in market discrimination. For example, they would be consistent if the employer class was heterogeneous in tastes, if all hired factors and consumers were homogeneous, if each firm had a vertical supply curve, and if employer discrimination was only a small part of market discrimination. Doubling the relative supply of non-whites would greatly increase employer discrimination but would have only a small effect on market discrimination.[15]

---

for discrimination against these groups. The average ratio of the MDC in the South to that in the North is 1.9, and this is taken as the average ratio of tastes for discrimination. This estimate is only a first approximation for these reasons: (1) The effect of proportions is underestimated, and the regional difference in tastes is overestimated because of the random errors of measurement. (2) There is no systematic tendency for the average size of establishment in each industry to differ between the North and the South. If tastes for discrimination were the same in both regions, this would suggest that the average value of R was about the same. However, since discrimination is greater in the South, southern producers have an incentive to specialize in industries with relatively small productive units (see pp. 87–88 for evidence of this), thereby reducing the average value of R there. (3) On the other hand, discrimination reduces the wage rate of non-whites relative to factors working with them, thereby increasing the value of R. These two changes are in opposite directions; therefore, the net regional difference in R produced by the regional difference in discrimination is not so large (absolutely) as the difference produced by either change separately.

15. Other assumptions could also produce consistent results. Suppose that each firm had a production function homogeneous of first degree, that employer discrimination was a very large part of market discrimination, and that all employers had the same tastes for discrimination—except for a few who had much smaller ones. A change in the relative supply of non-whites would not affect market discrimination very much, but discrimination in competitive industries would still be much less than in monopolistic ones. However, if the analyses are to be consistent, it is incorrect to believe both that a change in the relative supply of non-whites would greatly increase employer discrimination and that their discrimination would be a large part of market discrimination.

3. THE INFLUENCE OF THE NUMBER OF NON-WHITES
   ON DISCRIMINATION

The conclusion that a regional difference in tastes for discrimination exists "explains" the regional difference in market discrimination but introduces a new problem of "explaining" the difference in tastes. Many explanations emphasize the institutionalization in the South of the ill feeling against Negroes caused by slavery and the losses suffered from the Civil War.[16] I should like to investigate a different hypothesis, also mentioned in the literature;[17] these two hypotheses are related but suggest different empirical methods. The one used here assumes that tastes for discrimination against non-whites vary directly with their proportion in a community; consequently, discrimination against non-whites is greater in southern communities because relatively more of them live there.

One obstacle to an empirical investigation of this hypothesis is the difficulty in finding an appropriate measure of "community." Is an individual's discrimination determined primarily by the relative number of non-whites working with him in the same plant or by their relative numbers in his community, county, state, region, or some more complicated sociogeographical area? It seemed best to limit the discussion to individuals living in Standard Metropolitan Areas (SMA) as classified by the U.S. Census Bureau and to investigate whether their discrimination is influenced by the proportion of non-whites in the same SMA.

Columns 2 and 3 of Table 12 give the median incomes of white and Negro males in 1949 for all SMA's in the South. Column 4 gives the proportional difference between these incomes, and column 5 gives the percentage of non-whites in each SMA. The correlation coefficient between the numbers in columns 4 and 5 is $+0.73$ (and the coefficient of determination is 0.53).

One interpretation of this result is that tastes for discrimination and thus market discrimination are positively associated with the percentage of non-whites in each SMA. Before accepting this interpretation, it is necessary to separate the income differentials caused

16. Of the literally hundreds of sources that can be cited, see Gunnar Myrdal, *The American Dilemma* (New York: Harper & Bros., 1944), chap. xxviii.

17. See the references in n. 7.

TABLE 12

Relative Number, Income, and Education of Non-Whites for Standard Metropolitan Areas in the South in 1950*

Standard Metropolitan Area (1)	Median Income of White Males (2)	Median Income of Negro Males (3)	White Minus Negro Divided by Negro Col. 2 − Col. 3/Col. 3 (4)	Number of Non-Whites as a Percentage of Total (5)	Median Schooling of Non-Whites Divided by Median Schooling of Whites (6)
Asheville, N.C......	$2,156	$1,417	0.52	12.3	75.0
Atlanta, Ga.........	2,801	1,457	0.92	24.7	59.6
Augusta, Ga........	2,154	1,148	0.88	34.6	52.6
Austin, Tex.........	2,109	1,189	0.77	14.1	64.7
Baltimore, Md......	2,957	1,864	0.59	19.9	78.0
Baton Rouge, La....	3,508	1,420	1.47	33.1	43.8
Beaumont–Port Arthur, Tex.........	3,561	1,778	1.00	22.7	57.0
Birmingham, Ala..	2,883	1,676	0.72	37.3	59.3
Charleston, S.C.....	2,535	991	1.56	41.5	45.0
Charleston, W.Va....	2,802	2,081	0.35	8.4	93.2
Charlotte, N.C......	2,860	1,493	0.92	25.4	54.7
Chattanooga, Tenn..	2,278	1,527	0.49	18.2	74.4
Columbia, S.C......	2,528	1,152	1.19	35.4	50.9
Columbus, Ga.......	2,032	1,169	0.74	31.5	51.0
Corpus Christi, Tex..	2,455	1,665	0.47	4.9	79.4
Dallas, Tex.........	2,974	1,503	0.98	13.6	63.9
Durham, N.C.......	2,412	1,501	0.61	33.3	63.1
El Paso, Tex........	2,162	1,640	0.32	2.4	90.3
Fort Worth, Tex.....	2,777	1,503	0.85	11.0	69.9
Galveston, Tex......	3,152	1,757	0.79	21.1	71.6
Greensboro-Highpoint, N.C........	2,398	1,448	0.66	19.5	75.3
Greenville, S.C......	2,334	1,233	0.89	18.7	60.4
Houston, Tex........	3,255	1,803	0.81	18.7	68.5
Huntington, W.Va.⎱ Ashland, Ky. ⎰.	2,316	1,644	0.41	2.9	94.3
Jackson, Miss.......	2,883	1,120	1.57	45.0	51.6
Jacksonville, Fla.....	2,771	1,480	0.87	26.9	58.4
Knoxville, Tenn.....	2,229	1,555	0.43	7.8	80.9
Lexington, Ky.......	2,295	1,353	0.70	17.3	69.0
Little Rock–North Little Rock, Ark...	2,551	1,211	1.12	24.1	67.9
Louisville, Ky.......	2,790	1,723	0.62	11.5	88.0

* Source: Columns 2, 3, and 5 were obtained from U.S. Bureau of the Census, *Census of Population, 1950: U.S. Summary* (Washington, D.C.: Government Printing Office, 1953), Vol. II, Part 1, Tables 185, 86. Column 6 was estimated from U.S. Bureau of the Census, *Census of Population, 1950: State Reports* (Washington, D.C.: Government Printing Office, 1953), Vol. II, Tables 34 and 36. Individuals reporting no schooling were omitted, since errors of reporting are likely to be large for this group. Columns 5 and 6 refer to all non-whites, while col. 3 refers only to Negroes; in the South Negroes are an overwhelmingly large proportion of all non-whites.

TABLE 12—*Continued*

Standard Metropolitan Area (1)	Median Income of White Males (2)	Median Income of Negro Males (3)	White Minus Negro Divided by Negro Col. 2 − Col. 3/Col. 3 (4)	Number of Non-Whites as a Percentage of Total (5)	Median Schooling of Non-Whites Divided by Median Schooling of Whites (6)
Lubbock, Tex.......	$2,511	$1,307	0.92	7.9	61.9
Macon, Ga.........	2,608	1,159	1.25	35.7	49.0
Memphis, Tenn.....	2,892	1,401	1.06	37.4	56.3
Miami, Fla.........	2,776	1,654	0.68	13.2	54.6
Mobile, Ala........	2,609	1,314	0.99	33.8	59.6
Montgomery, Ala....	2,791	1,034	1.70	43.6	49.2
Nashville, Tenn.....	2,490	1,353	0.84	20.0	73.8
New Orleans, La.....	2,621	1,459	0.80	29.3	68.1
Norfolk-Portsmouth, Va........	2,590	1,591	0.63	27.5	61.5
Oklahoma City, Okla.	2,773	1,729	0.60	8.6	73.1
Orlando, Fla........	2,293	1,202	0.91	19.8	52.5
Raleigh, N.C........	2,274	1,217	0.87	29.3	60.0
Richmond, Va.......	2,996	1,585	0.89	26.6	63.1
Roanoke, Va........	2,747	1,773	0.55	13.6	76.0
San Antonio, Tex....	2,080	1,521	0.37	6.7	91.3
Savannah, Ga.......	2,759	1,291	1.14	38.6	53.3
Shreveport, La......	3,166	1,121	1.82	37.6	41.5
Tampa–St. Petersburg, Fla.........	2,137	1,376	0.55	13.9	57.4
Tulsa, Okla.........	2,916	1,530	0.91	9.1	71.7
Waco, Tex.........	2,235	1,051	1.13	17.2	72.7
Washington, D.C....	3,407	2,137	0.59	23.4	69.4
Wilmington, Del.....	3,107	1,892	0.64	12.0	70.8
Winston-Salem, N.C.	2,447	1,507	0.64	28.4	70.1

by discrimination from those caused by differences in economic capacity. Column 6 gives the ratio of the median years of schooling of non-whites to whites, and a comparison of columns 5 and 6 shows that the relative education of non-whites tends to be low in SMA's where they are present in relatively large numbers. This suggests that the negative association between relative income and numbers may have been caused by the negative association between relative education and numbers. This can be tested by finding the partial correlation coefficient between the observations in columns 4 and 5, holding those in column 6 constant. The value of this coefficient is $+0.31$ (and the partial coefficient of determination is 0.09). Although it is significantly different from zero at the 0.05

level, the effect of proportions on relative incomes has been substantially reduced, since it now explains only 9 per cent of the variation in relative incomes. The proportion of non-whites in a SMA does not seem to have an important effect on tastes for discrimination that operate through the market.[18]

Proportions seem to have a strong effect on tastes for discrimination that operate through non-market channels. The simple correlation coefficient between the observations in columns 5 and 6 is −0.79, and the partial correlation coefficient between these observations, holding those in column 4 constant, is −0.45. The relative education of non-whites thus tends to be low in SMA's where they are most numerous; since most education is publicly administered, this suggests that in the South political discrimination against non-whites is positively associated with their relative number.[19]

18. The crudeness of the data subjects this conclusion to much error. No adjustment was made for variation in the relative age of non-whites among different SMA's. This omission may not be very serious, since the variation in relative age is rather small and much less than the variation in education. The crude measure of education is another source of error; a more refined analysis would include a measure of dispersion in education. A major error may arise because wage and salary income is combined with capital income. As far as I am aware, lack of data makes it impossible to separate wages and salaries from returns on capital.

It would be desirable to compute a partial correlation coefficient between relative income and proportions, holding relative education constant, for all SMA's in the North and the South. Unfortunately, the 1950 Census gives no racial breakdown of the educational data for northern SMA's. The simple correlation coefficient in northern SMA's between relative incomes and proportions is only +0.29 (and the coefficient of determination is 0.09). This coefficient is lower than that obtained for the South (+0.73) partly because the variation in proportion of non-whites in different SMA's is much less in the North.

19. This negative association between relative education and relative numbers has also been noted by C. A. Anderson, "Inequalities in Schooling in the South," *American Journal of Sociology*, LX (May, 1955), 557. Different evidence likewise suggesting a positive association between political discrimination and relative numbers has been presented by A. Heard, *A Two-Party South* (Chapel Hill: University of North Carolina Press, 1952).

Column 6 refers to the education of individuals living in a SMA; since they may have received their education elsewhere, these data do not necessarily give an accurate picture of the educational facilities provided. However, Anderson (*op. cit.*, pp. 560–61) presents evidence which indicates that the education of those living in a SMA is a good index of the education provided.

ADDENDUM TO CHAPTER 8

Absolute income differentials between college and high-school graduates are substantially less for non-whites than for whites: for example, in 1939 non-white male college graduates aged 35–44 earned about $700 more in the South and $500 more in the North than non-white high-school graduates, about one-third of the $2,000 differential for whites. Non-whites do not necessarily gain less from college, however, since both their direct and indirect college costs are much lower. Indirect costs are lower because non-white high-school graduates earn less than white graduates, and direct costs are lower because non-whites attend cheaper (and "lower-quality") colleges.[20] Again the relevant question is whether the difference in costs is sufficient to compensate for the difference in returns. Depending on the adjustments for taxes and growth, the 1939 cohort of urban, non-white, male college graduates received rates of return ranging from 10.6 to 14 per cent in the South, and from 6.6 to 10 per cent in the North, with the best estimates at about 12.3 and 8.3 per cent.[21] Both are less than the 14.5 per cent

Addendum reprinted with minor changes from Gary Becker, *Human Capital* (New York: Columbia University Press, 1964), pp. 94–100.

20. Most non-whites are Negroes and about 85 per cent of Negro college students in 1947 were enrolled in Negro colleges. See *Higher Education for American Democracy, A Report of the President's Commission on Higher Education* (Washington, 1947), Vol. II, p. 31. In 1940 the average expenditure per student in Negro colleges was only about 70 per cent of that in white colleges. For white costs, see Commission on Financing Higher Education, *Current Operating Expenditures and Income of Higher Education in the United States, 1930, 1940 and 1950* (New York, 1952), Tables 58 and 3; for Negro costs, see "Statistics of Higher Education, 1939–40," *Biennial Survey of Education in the U.S., 1938–40* (Washington, 1944), Vol. II, Chap. 4, Tables 18 and 19. For some complaints about the low quality of Negro colleges, see the article by F. M. Hechinger in the *New York Times*, September 22, 1963.

21. All non-white graduates are assumed to go to Negro colleges, which was nearly true of non-whites in the South and largely true of those in the North. If northern non-whites went to white colleges, their rate of return would only be about 7.3 per cent.

rate for urban native-white males.[22] This evidence indicates that non-white male high-school graduates have less incentive than white graduates, but not much less, to go to college.

One way to check such a conclusion, as well as to provide indirect evidence on rates of return when direct evidence is not available, is to look at actual behavior. Each group of high-school graduates can be said to have a curve relating the fraction going to college to the gain expected from college. Presumably these curves are positively inclined, and their location and elasticity are determined, respectively, by the average level and the dispersion around the average in ability, availability of financing, tastes, and attitudes toward risk. If two groups had identical supply curves, the gain expected by one would be larger if, and only if, the fraction going to college were also larger.

Now if white and non-white males had identical supply curves, the modestly higher rate of return estimated for whites would imply—if the elasticity was of medium size—that a modestly larger fraction of whites would go to college.[23] Many readers may be surprised to learn that almost the same percentage of non-white high-school graduates go to college as white: in 1957, about one-third of all non-white male high-school graduates over 25 had some college, while a little over two-fifths of all white male graduates did.[24] Of course, the fact that fewer non-whites go to college cannot be considered impressive support of the evidence indicating that non-whites gain less. For their supply curve has probably been to

22. None of these rates have been adjusted for differential ability because the relevant data are not available for non-whites. Their *differential* ability is probably greater than that for whites because only the more ambitious and otherwise able non-whites can overcome their very low socioeconomic background and go on to college. If so, adjusted rates would be relatively lower for non-whites.

23. Of course, the quantity supplied would be a function of the expected real gain, not merely the monetary gain. In relating relative supplies to relative monetary gains, I am implicitly assuming that any differences in psychic gains can be ignored. See *Human Capital*, Chap. 5 for a further discussion of psychic gains and their relation to actual behavior.

24. See *Population Characteristics, Educational Attainment: March 1957*, Tables 1 and 3.

the left of that of whites,[25] and thus fewer non-whites would go to college even if the gains were the same. But the relatively small difference in the fractions going to college is impressive support of the evidence indicating that the difference in gains is not very great. For *many fewer* non-whites would go to college if their supply curve were much to the left *and* if they gained much less from college.[26]

It may be surprising that the rate of return to non-white college graduates appears lower in the North than in the South and only slightly lower than the rate of return to whites, since discrimination is clearly much greater in the South and increases in both regions with the education of non-whites. In this section, rate of return estimates are related to the analysis of discrimination, thus reconciling the findings here with the analysis in chapter 8 of discrimination. The main result of this reconciliation is to support the implications of the rate of return estimates; namely, discrimination against non-white college graduates may have been less in the South than in the North and relatively modest, especially in the South.

The market discrimination coefficient (MDC) between two groups has been defined as

$$MDC = \frac{\pi_u}{\pi_n} - \frac{\pi_w^0}{\pi_n^0}, \qquad (A1)$$

where π_w and π_n are actual earnings and π_w^0 and π_n^0 are what they would be in the absence of market discrimination. If these groups

25. Non-whites typically have less resources, and experience greater difficulty in gaining admission to certain colleges.

26. Moreover, there is some evidence that fewer non-white male graduates generally go to college even when father's education and several other variables are held constant. See *School Enrollment, and Education of Young Adults and Their Fathers: October 1960*, Current Population Reports (Washington, 1961), Table 9; and Bureau of the Census, *Factors Related to College Attendance of Farm and Nonfarm High School Graduates: 1960* (Washington, 1962), Table 16. In general, non-whites have been found to have less education even when many other factors are held constant. See M. H. David, H. Brazer, J. Morgan, and W. Cohen, *Educational Achievement: Its Causes and Effects* (Ann Arbor, 1961), Tables 1–10.

were equally productive, $\pi_n^0 = \pi_w^0$, and

$$MDC = \frac{\pi_w}{\pi_n} - 1 \,. \tag{A2}$$

If several sets of these groups can be distinguished by an ordered characteristic, such as occupation, education, age, or income, the *MDC* can be said to measure average discrimination, and a marginal *MDC* measuring the additional discrimination encountered as a result of moving to a higher level can be defined in terms of the change in earnings between levels, as:

$$MDC_{ij} = \frac{\pi_w^j - \pi_w^i}{\pi_n^j - \pi_n^i} - \frac{\pi_w^{0j} - \pi_w^{0i}}{\pi_n^{0j} - \pi_n^{0i}} \,, \tag{A3}$$

where j and i are different levels of the characteristic in question. Equal productivity between W and N would give the simpler relation

$$MDC_{ij} = \frac{\pi_w^j - \pi_w^i}{\pi_n^j - \pi_n^i} - 1 \,. \tag{A4}$$

Well-known relations between marginal and average functions imply that the marginal *MDC* would be above, equal to, or less than the average *MDC* depending on whether the latter was increasing, constant, or decreasing.

Columns 1–3 of the table measure the average and columns 4 and 5 the marginal *MDC* at various ages in 1939 between white and non-white elementary, high-school, and college graduates, assuming that non-whites and whites are really equally productive. In the North both marginals tend to be above the corresponding averages, while in the South they are somewhat below at the college level.

These marginal *MDC*'s measure the ratio of the returns from additional schooling to whites and non-whites,[27] and are greater,

27. According to equation (A4), the marginal *MDC* at a particular age would be

$$MDC_{ij} = \frac{\pi_{wj} - \pi_{wi}}{\pi_{nj} - \pi_{ni}} - 1 \,,$$

$$= \frac{\Delta\pi_{wij}}{\Delta\pi_{nij}} - 1 \,,$$

equal to, or less than zero as the return to whites is greater, equal to, or less than that to non-whites. The previous discussion indicated that the return from college is lower for non-whites partly because both their costs and their incremental benefits are lower. To the extent that returns differ because of cost differences, they do not measure market discrimination alone; rather they measure the combined effects of market and non-market discrimination.

TABLE 12A

AVERAGE AND MARGINAL MARKET DISCRIMINATION AGAINST
NON-WHITES FOR VARIOUS AGE AND EDUCATION
CLASSES, BY REGION, 1939

AGE	AVERAGE *MDC* BY YEARS OF EDUCATION			MARGINAL *MDC* BY YEARS OF EDUCATION		ADJUSTED MARGINAL *MDC* BY YEARS OF EDUCATION	
	16+ (1)	12 (2)	7 & 8 (3)	16+ (4)	12 (5)	16+ (6)	12 (7)
	SOUTH						
25–29....	.82	1.08	.69	.35	4.35	.37	3.57
30–34....	1.27	1.23	.89	1.33	2.97	.43	2.65
35–44....	1.50	1.68	1.12	1.23	4.49	.61	3.66
45–54....	1.57	1.62	1.27	1.49	2.85	.69	2.57
55–64....	1.56	1.55	1.08	1.62	3.61	.72	3.07
	NORTH						
25–29....	.47	.50	.37	.37	1.23	.71	1.52
30–34....	.78	.72	.45	.89	2.82	.99	2.61
35–44....	1.17	.96	.64	1.75	2.70	1.44	2.53
45–54....	1.37	.85	.73	3.92	1.17	2.58	1.48
55–64....	1.23	.70	.63	5.11	.86	3.20	1.27

Source: Basic data from *16th Census of the United States: 1940, Population, Educational Attainment by Economic Characteristics and Marital Status*, Bureau of the Census (Washington, 1947), Tables 29, 31, 33, 35. Zeman (in his unpublished Ph.D. dissertation, "A Quantitative Analysis of White-Non-White Income Differentials") computed mean incomes from these data for whites and non-whites by region, age, and education class. The average, marginal, and adjusted *MDC*'s are all defined and discussed in the text.

where π_{wi} and π_{wj} are the incomes of whites at two schooling levels, and π_{ni} and π_{nj} are the incomes of non-whites. But $\Delta\pi_{wij}$ and $\Delta\pi_{nij}$ are simply the returns to whites and non-whites, respectively, from going from the ith to the jth school level.

The more general definition in equation (A3) tries to correct for these influences by subtracting from the observed differentials those differences that would exist were there no marginal market discrimination. The empirical implementation of such a correction is always difficult;[28] a simple approach is to assume that if there were no marginal market discrimination, whites and non-whites would receive the same rate of return on their additional schooling. Their respective costs are taken as given, although in reality they may differ because of non-market discrimination and other factors.[29] With this approach, the marginal *MDC* becomes proportional to the percentage difference in rates of return, the factor of proportionality being the ratio of costs.[30] So the rate of return and market discrimination approaches come more or less to the same thing when a distinction is drawn between marginal and average discrimination.

28. See the discussion in Chap. 8.

29. One such factor is market discrimination at lower age and educational levels since the lower foregone earnings of non-white college students result partly from market discrimination against non-white elementary and high-school graduates. Consequently, this approach implies that market discrimination at lower levels reduces the earnings that non-white college graduates would receive even if there were no discrimination against non-white *college graduates*. This implication may or may not be considered reasonable, but for my purposes it is not necessary to use a more sophisticated method.

30. The marginal discrimination coefficient can be written as

$$MDC_{ij} = \frac{\Delta \pi_w}{\Delta \pi_n} - \frac{\Delta \pi_w^0}{\Delta \pi_n^0}.$$

To a first approximation

$$\Delta \pi_w = r_w C_w \text{ and } \Delta \pi_n = r_n C_n ,$$

where r_w and r_n are the rates of return and C_w and C_n are the costs of moving from the ith to the jth educational level. By assumption,

$$\Delta \pi_w^0 = r C_w \text{ and } \Delta \pi_n^0 = r C_n .$$

Therefore, the first equation in the footnote can be written as

$$MDC_{ij} = \frac{r_w C_w}{r_n C_n} - \frac{r C_w}{r C_n}$$

$$= \frac{C_w}{C_n} \left(\frac{r_w - r_n}{r_n} \right).$$

Consequently, since the rate of return to non-white college graduates is much higher in the South than in the North, the adjusted marginal *MDC* should be much lower there.[31] Moreover, the rather small difference between the rate of return to whites and to southern non-whites implies that the adjusted *MDC* in the South should be quite small, certainly much smaller than the average and the unadjusted marginal *MDC*'s against college graduates. Column 6, which assumes that non-white college graduates would have received the same rate of return as white graduates were there no market discrimination against them, supports these implications: the adjusted marginal *MDC* is only about .6 in the South compared to 1.4 in the North and to average and unadjusted marginal *MDC*'s in the South of 1.5 and 1.2, respectively.

Market discrimination against southern non-white college graduates is apparently relatively small, even though market discrimination against non-whites is generally quite large in the South.[32] One possible line of explanation emphasizes that non-white college graduates partially avoid white discrimination by catering to their own market, where the discrimination against them is presumably less severe. A relatively large fraction of non-white college graduates were, indeed, in occupations that cater to a segregated market: in 1940 about 50 per cent of non-white graduates were doctors, dentists, clergymen, teachers, or lawyers, while only 35 per cent of white graduates were engaged in these professions.[33] The opportunities to

31. This conclusion presupposes that the rate of return to white college graduates is also not much higher in the South. The available evidence suggests that the rate of return to whites is somewhat higher in the South.

32. The 1950 Census also shows larger earning differentials between college and high-school non-whites in the South than in North (see C. A. Anderson, "Regional and Racial Differences in Relations between Income and Education," *The School Review*, January 1955, pp. 38–46). The 1950 Census data, however, did not separate rural from urban persons, and many more southern than northern non-whites live in rural areas, especially at lower educational levels. Perhaps this explains why the 1950 Census, unlike the 1940 Census, also shows larger differentials in the South between non-whites with high-school and elementary school educations.

33. See Bureau of the Census, *1940 Census of Population, Occupational Characteristics* (sample statistics) (Washington, 1943), Table 3.

cater to a segregated market were probably more available to southern graduates since the non-white market is both larger (relative to supply) and more segregated there.[34] Fewer opportunities to avoid discrimination are available to non-white high-school graduates: the same fraction of whites and non-whites were in occupations not catering to segregated markets.[35] This would explain why column 7, which presents adjusted marginal MDC's against non-white high-school graduates, shows substantially greater discrimination in the South.

Let me emphasize, however, in concluding this section, that a much more intensive examination of the evidence, especially of that collected in the 1960 and 1970 Censuses, is necessary before these findings can be fully accepted.

34. For a discussion of evidence on income distributions that led to the same interpretation, see Milton Friedman, *A Theory of the Consumption Function* (Princeton: NBER, 1957), pp. 84–85.

35. For example, in 1940 about 37 per cent of both white and non-white high-school graduates were craftsmen, operators, or laborers, occupational groups which do not sell their services to segregated markets. (See *1940 Census of Population, Occupational Characteristics*, Table 3.)

CHAPTER NINE

Changes in Discrimination over Time

The passage of time has been accompanied by changes in other variables, which may have changed the amount of discrimination. An important secular increase in real income per capita has occurred in the United States during the last hundred years, and it would be interesting to know whether this increased or decreased the "consumption" of discrimination. The continual rise in the educational attainments of the United States population would be relevant if there were a significant correlation between discrimination and educational level.[1]

There has been a secular increase in the activities of organizations dedicated to eliminating discrimination, and this may have affected tastes. The rapid growth of the federal government may have had important consequences for discrimination against minority groups. In the last fifty years the United States has passed through two major wars, one major depression, and several periods of expansion and contraction, and these, too, may have left their mark on the extent and direction of discrimination. Other changes, such as in the regional distribution of different groups, in the amount of immigration, or in the underlying technology, may also be relevant for a study of discrimination.

The almost total lack of income data for minority groups before the 1930's prevents any real study of the separate influence of each

1. It was shown in the last chapter that discrimination in 1940 was greater against non-whites in higher education categories, but this does not imply greater discrimination by whites in higher categories.

of these changes.[2] It is possible, however, to learn something about the secular change in discrimination. Probably the best statistics for this purpose are those in the United States Census reports giving, for each census year since 1890, the occupations of persons gainfully employed (or in the labor force), with a sex and color breakdown. These occupational statistics contain important information about the absolute and relative changes in the economic position of Negroes.

Our knowledge of the absolute and relative occupational distribution of Negro slaves is extremely limited. Since slaves were one form of capital, investment in them was carried to the point at which marginal costs equaled marginal gains; this view offers no reason to expect the occupational position of slaves to have been inferior to that of free Negroes and whites. On the other hand, slaves differed from other capital, since they could work with varying degrees of intensity; this often made slave labor unsuitable for certain occupations, especially the more skilled ones. Very few (if any) Negro slaves received training for occupations requiring much formal education, such as medicine and law. This is not surprising if formal education was accompanied by aspirations for freedom, which, in turn, would reduce the productivity of educated slaves. Indeed, in many southern states there were laws prohibiting whites from teaching their slaves how to read and write.

The earliest detailed and inclusive occupational statistics for Negroes and whites located for this study were those in the 1890 Census; the data for this year are presented in Table 13 in the two categories of skilled and unskilled workers.[3] By 1890, the proportion

2. The one important exception is the rather substantial time series on male and female wage rates and incomes. No attempt has been made to analyze these differentials here because they have been studied by H. Sanborne in "Pay Differences between Men and Women," *Industrial and Labor Relations Review*, Vol. 17 (July 1964), pp. 534–50.

3. Semiskilled workers were not separated from unskilled before the 1910 Census. In deriving the figures in Table 13 the census occupation called "farmers and farm tenants" was omitted. It is extremely difficult to compare or classify the skills of whites and Negroes in this occupation, since most Negroes in it are farm tenants and most whites are farm owners (see U.S. Bureau of the Census, *United States Census of Agriculture, 1950, Color, Race, Tenure of Farm Operators* [Washington, D.C.: Government Printing Office, 1952], p. 924).

of Negroes in skilled occupations was substantially less than that of whites. Although it is possible that this difference can be completely explained by the changes between 1865 and 1890, a more plausible inference would be that the proportion of slaves in skilled occupations was much less than that of whites. This would support the previous statement that slave labor is relatively unproductive in the more skilled occupations.

TABLE 13

RELATIVE NUMBER OF NEGRO AND WHITE MALES IN DIFFERENT
OCCUPATIONAL CATEGORIES FOR THE UNITED STATES
1890–1950*

YEAR	RELATIVE NUMBER IN SKILLED OCCUPATIONS†			RELATIVE NUMBER IN SEMISKILLED OCCUPATIONS†			RELATIVE NUMBER IN UNSKILLED OCCUPATIONS†		
	White	Negro	White Divided by Negro	White	Negro	White Divided by Negro	White	Negro	White Divided by Negro
(1)	(2)	(3)	(4)	(5)	(6)	(7)	(8)	(9)	(10)
1950.......	0.597	0.193	3.093	0.230	0.249	0.923	0.174	0.558	0.311
1940.......	.528	.129	4.084	.218	.159	1.368	.255	.712	.358
1930.......	.531	.118	4.486	.174	.115	1.512	.295	.767	.385
1920.......	.501	.109	4.579	.168	.098	1.803	.333	.798	.417
1910.......	.461	.092	4.999	.146	.064	2.301	.393	.844	.466
1900.......	.431	.071	6.065	‡	‡	‡	.569	.929	.613
1890.......	0.443	0.071	6.279	‡	‡	‡	0.557	0.929	0.599

* Source: See the appendix to this chapter (pp. 142–47).

† The "relative number" of Negroes in a particular occupational category means the number of Negro males in this category divided by the total number of gainfully occupied Negro males (excluding farmers and farm tenants); a similar definition is used here for whites.

‡ Combined with unskilled.

It is clear from columns 2 and 3 that there were relatively fewer skilled Negroes than whites in each census year from 1890 to 1950; it is also clear from columns 5 and 6 that there were relatively fewer semiskilled Negroes from 1910 to 1940 and slightly more in 1950. These data show that Negroes have been lower in the occupational hierarchy than whites. The average occupational level of Negroes has, however, been rising steadily over time; for example, in 1950, 19 per cent of all Negroes were skilled and 25 per cent were semiskilled, as against only 7 per cent skilled in 1890 and 6 per cent semiskilled in 1910.

Some might conjecture that this advance resulted from the steady movement of Negroes out of the South (see Table 14), since the occupational distribution of Negroes is higher in the North. Table 15 gives the occupational distribution of whites and Negroes in the North and South in 1910, 1940, and 1950. Columns 3 and 6

TABLE 14

NUMBER OF NEGROES AND WHITES IN THE
NORTH AND SOUTH, 1890–1950*

YEAR	SOUTH			NORTH		
	Whites (in Millions)	Negroes (in Millions)	Negroes Divided by Whites	Whites (in Millions)	Negroes (in Millions)	Negroes Divided by Whites
1950........	36.8	10.2	0.28	98.1	4.8	0.049
1940........	31.7	9.9	.31	86.6	3.0	.034
1930........	28.4	9.4	.33	81.9	2.5	.031
1920........	24.1	8.9	.37	70.7	1.6	.022
1910........	20.5	8.7	.43	61.2	1.1	.018
1900........	16.5	7.9	.48	50.3	0.9	.018
1890........	13.2	6.8	0.51	41.9	0.7	0.017

* Source: 1890–1910, U.S. Bureau of the Census, *Negro Population, 1790–1915* (Washington, D.C.: Government Printing Office, 1918), p. 43; 1920–40, U.S. Bureau of the Census, *Statistical Abstract of the United States, 1952* (Washington, D.C.: Government Printing Office, 1952), p. 32; 1950, U.S. Bureau of the Census, *Census of Population, 1950* (Washington, D.C.: Government Printing Office, 1953), II, 1–106.

show that the proportion of Negroes in skilled and semiskilled occupations has been consistently higher in the North than in the South. These columns also show that the average occupational position of Negroes has risen over time within both the North and the South. However, comparisons of column 2 with column 3 and of column 5 with column 6 show conclusively that in both regions Negroes have always had a much lower position on the occupational ladder.

It can be seen from columns 2 and 5 that the average occupational position of whites has also risen over time, and this leads to the question whether the average Negro position has risen primarily because of the impact of such forces as a general increase in education, which increases the position of all groups, or because of such forces, as a decrease in discrimination, which increases the relative position of Negroes. A numerical measure of occupational position is needed in order to determine the relative change in the position of Negroes.

Occupational position can probably be measured best by the average wage and salary income received by whites in each skill category. Zeman estimated the incomes received by whites in 1940 in different census occupational categories in the North and South; these estimates suggest that the relative position of skilled, semi-

TABLE 15

RELATIVE NUMBER OF NEGRO AND WHITE MALES IN DIFFERENT OCCUPATIONAL CATEGORIES FOR THE NORTH AND SOUTH
1910, 1940, 1950*

YEAR	RELATIVE NUMBER IN SKILLED OCCUPATIONS†			RELATIVE NUMBER IN SEMISKILLED OCCUPATIONS†			RELATIVE NUMBER IN UNSKILLED OCCUPATIONS†		
	White	Negro	White Divided by Negro	White	Negro	White Divided by Negro	White	Negro	White Divided by Negro
(1)	(2)	(3)	(4)	(5)	(6)	(7)	(8)	(9)	(10)
North									
1950.......	0.597	0.245	2.433	0.237	0.297	0.798	0.167	0.458	0.364
1940‡.....	.538	.181	2.973	.232	.214	1.083	.230	.605	.381
1910.......	0.472	0.135	3.504	0.162	0.136	1.195	0.366	0.730	0.501
South									
1950.......	0.597	0.162	3.683	0.208	0.221	0.942	0.195	0.617	0.316
1940‡.....	.513	.097	5.304	.195	.151	1.296	.292	.753	.388
1910.......	0.411	0.080	5.126	0.071	0.043	1.657	0.518	0.877	0.591

* Source: See the appendix to this chapter (p. 148).

† The relative number of Negroes or whites in a particular occupational category is defined in Table 13.

‡ The relative number of skilled Negroes is probably slightly understated and the relative number of semiskilled Negroes slightly overstated for 1940 (see the appendix to this chapter).

skilled, and unskilled occupations can be represented by 2.34, 1.44, and 1.00 in the North and by 2.69, 1.49, and 1.00 in the South.[4] The application of these weights to the distribution data in Table 15 yields the occupational indexes of Table 16. The indexes in columns 2, 3, 5, and 6 show that in both regions the average occupational position of Negroes and whites rose between 1910 and 1940 and between 1940 and 1950. However, the relative position of Negroes (given in columns 4 and 7) has been remarkably stable over time.[5]

TABLE 16

AN INDEX OF THE OCCUPATIONAL POSITION OF NEGROES AND WHITES
IN THE NORTH AND SOUTH FOR 1910, 1940, AND 1950

YEAR (1)	NORTH			SOUTH		
	Whites (2)	Negroes (3)	Negroes Divided by Whites (4)	Whites (5)	Negroes (6)	Negroes Divided by Whites (7)
1950........	1.90	1.46	0.77	2.11	1.38	0.65
1940........	1.82	1.34	.74	1.96	1.24	.63
1910........	1.70	1.24	0.73	1.73	1.16	0.67

In both the North and the South the maximum deviation from the average was less than 6 per cent. In the North there was very little change from 1910 to 1940 and a 4 per cent increase between 1940 and 1950; in the South there was a 6 per cent decrease from

4. Zeman's estimates can be found in "A Quantitative Analysis of White–Non-white Income Differentials in the United States in 1939" (unpublished Ph.D. dissertation, Department of Economics, University of Chicago, 1955), Appendix D. The average wage and salary income of white professional workers, proprietors and officials, clerical and sales workers, and foremen and craftsmen was used as the average income of skilled whites; the wage and salary income of white operatives as the income of semiskilled whites; and the wage and salary income of white laborers as the income of unskilled whites.

5. Dewey, in "Negro Employment in Southern Industry," *Journal of Political Economy*, LX (August, 1952), *passim*, argues that in the last forty or fifty years Negroes have advanced little relative to whites in the occupational hierarchy in the South. These data not only support Dewey's observations but also show that the same is true for the North.

1910 to 1940 and a 4 per cent increase between 1940 and 1950. Thus, in comparing 1950 with 1910, Negroes in the North had about a 5 per cent higher relative occupational position and in the South about a 2 per cent lower position.[6]

In answer to the earlier question, it seems that almost all the increase in the absolute occupational position of Negroes was caused by forces increasing the position of whites as well. Changes in variables affecting the relative position of Negroes presumably either were minor or offset one another. A large secular decrease in discrimination against Negroes could have occurred only if changes in other variables offset its effect.[7] Since it is difficult to think of individual changes that could have greatly lowered their relative position, it seems probable that a large secular decrease in discrimination did not occur; yet it is possible that the combined effects of many small changes, such as a decrease in the number of unskilled whites immigrating from abroad, were great enough to offset a large decrease in discrimination.[8]

6. For some purposes it would be preferable to use the weights obtained for the North in constructing occupational indexes for the South as well, since northern white incomes were less affected by discrimination. When this is done, the absolute and relative occupational position of Negroes and Whites are as in the accompanying table. Negroes had a consistently lower position in the South

	1910	1940	1950
Whites....................	1.581	1.772	1.890
Negroes...................	1.126	1.195	1.314
Negroes divided by whites...	0.713	0.675	0.695

than in the North; whites had a lower position in the South in 1910 and 1940 and the same position in both areas in 1950. These weights imply a somewhat higher relative occupational position of southern Negroes than those used in Table 16, but the percentage changes in this position from 1910 to 1940 and from 1940 to 1950 are about the same.

7. A decrease in discrimination could increase merely the relative income of Negroes within an occupational category and not change their relative occupational distribution. However, since discrimination against Negroes has been greater in the more skilled occupations, a large decrease in discrimination would probably also increase their opportunities in these occupations.

8. The same considerations apply when estimating the likelihood that there was a large secular increase in discrimination.

APPENDIX TO CHAPTER 9

The census occupational statistics from 1890 to 1930 include all "gainful workers"; from 1940 to 1950 they include only members of the "labor force." Alba Edwards adjusted the labor-force statistics to make them comparable to those for gainful workers,[9] but, since the adjustment does not include any occupation, sex, or race breakdown, the unadjusted figures have been used.

Edwards' classifications[10] were used to combine occupations into socio-economic groups. There are six such groups: (1) professional persons; (2) proprietors, managers, and officials; (3) clerks and kindred workers; (4) skilled workers and foremen; (5) semiskilled workers; and (6) unskilled workers. All persons (excluding farmers and farm tenants) in each of the first four groups are classified as "skilled workers" in Tables 13 and 15. Although an attempt was made to allocate each occupational category to one of these groups, this was impossible for a few categories in certain years.

The occupations of persons ten to thirteen years of age are included in the statistics from 1890 to 1930; they are excluded for 1940 and 1950 because the data are not available. In 1920 about 260,000 males ten to thirteen years old were gainfully occupied; in 1930 only about 160,000.[11] The secular decrease in employment of children implies that no more than about 100,000 males ten to thirteen years of age were in the labor force in 1940. This number is too small to cause serious bias.

Members of the armed forces are included in semiskilled workers from 1890 to 1930. They are omitted for 1940 because World War II had started, and for 1950 because selective service was in operation.

9. Alba M. Edwards, *Comparative Occupation Statistics for the United States, 1870 to 1940* (Washington, D.C.: Government Printing Office, 1943), chap. iv. This will be referred to as "*Comparative.*"

10. Alba M. Edwards, *A Socio-economic Grouping of the Gainful Workers of the United States* (Washington, D.C.: Government Printing Office, 1938), pp. 3–6. This will be referred to as "*Socio-economic.*"

11. U.S. Bureau of the Census, *Census of Population, 1930* (Washington, D.C.: Government Printing Office, 1933), V, 114.

1. TABLE 13

a) 1950

The 1950 Census data give occupations of employed persons with a breakdown for sex and race.[12] Data giving the occupations of the experienced labor force would be more comparable to the occupational data found in earlier censuses;[13] but as yet there are no published data giving the usual occupation of unemployed persons by race. The omission of unemployed persons could not cause a serious bias, since, in 1950, only 4 per cent of all those in the experienced labor force were unemployed.[14]

The occupational classification for the 1950 Census differed slightly from the classification used by Edwards in obtaining socio-economic groupings; in this census, occupations at different socio-economic levels were sometimes reported together as a single "occupation." All workers in each of these "occupations" were allocated to the level at which a majority of them belonged. Fortunately, no significant bias could result, since very few males were misclassified.[15]

b) 1940

The statistics for 1940 in Table 13 are from the 5 per cent sample giving the present occupation of employed persons and the usual occupation of experienced unemployed and public emergency workers,[16] broken down as to white and non-white. Although it is diffi-

12. U.S. Bureau of the Census, *Census of Population, 1950* (Washington, D.C.: Government Printing Office, 1953), II, 276.

13. See Edwards, *Comparative*, p. 7.

14. *Census of Population, 1950*, Vol. II, Tables 52 and 53.

15. Males in the following occupations were misclassified: incorrectly classified as skilled: (1) factory painters (should have been semiskilled), (2) motion-picture projectors (should have been semiskilled); incorrectly classified as semiskilled: (1) coopers (should have been skilled), (2) heaters (should have been unskilled), (3) furnacemen (should have been unskilled), (4) railroad conductors (should have been skilled); incorrectly classified as unskilled: (1) Other service workers (about half should have been semiskilled).

16. U.S. Bureau of the Census, *Census of Population, 1940: Sample Statistics on Usual Occupations* (Washington, D.C.: Government Printing Office, 1943), Table 4.

cult to ascertain the exact bias resulting from using statistics of non-whites rather than Negroes, it cannot be very large, since Negroes were about 93 per cent of all non-whites.[17]

These are the statistics in the 1940 Census most comparable to the gainfully occupied statistics of the earlier censuses.[18] The 1940

TABLE 17

COMPARISON OF TWO SETS OF OCCUPATIONAL
DATA IN THE 1940 CENSUS*

KIND OF DATA	SKILLED OCCUPATIONS			SEMISKILLED OCCUPATIONS			UNSKILLED OCCUPATIONS		
	Whites	Non-Whites†	Whites Divided by Non-Whites	Whites	Non-Whites†	Whites Divided by Non-Whites	Whites	Non-Whites†	Whites Divided by Non-Whites
Usual occupation...	0.528	0.129	4.084	0.218	0.159	1.368	0.255	0.712	0.358
Last occupation...	0.532	0.120	4.438	0.224	0.168	1.332	0.244	0.712	0.343
Usual occupation divided by last occupation...	.....	.....	0.920	.....	.....	1.027	.....	.....	1.043

* Source: U.S. Bureau of the Census, *Census of Population, 1940: Sample Statistics on Usual Occupations* (Washington, D.C.: Government Printing Office, 1943), Table 4, and *Census of Population, 1940*, Vol. III, Table 62.

† The data on "Usual Occupation" refer to all non-whites; those on "Last Occupation" refer to Negroes.

Census also gives data on the present occupation of employed persons and the last occupation of the experienced unemployed, for whites and Negroes;[19] in Table 17 these data are compared with those giving "usual occupations." The largest difference occurs in the skilled category; the relative proportion of "non-whites" in this category was 8 per cent larger with the data giving usual occupations. Part of this difference could be explained if Negroes suffered

17. U.S. Department of Commerce, *Statistical Abstract of the United States, 1953* (Washington, D.C.: Government Printing Office, 1953), p. 35.

18. Edwards, *Comparative*, pp. 19–20.

19. U.S. Bureau of the Census, *Census of Population, 1940*, Vol. III, Table 62.

more from depressions than whites, and part could be a consequence of comparing the usual occupations of non-whites with the current and last occupations of Negroes.

In 1940, as in 1950, it was sometimes impossible to allocate all males to the correct socio-economic class. Fortunately, there were very few males misclassified, and no significant bias could result from this.[20]

The statistics in Table 17 are derived from data in the 1940 Census. Edwards has pointed out that occupational statistics

TABLE 18

COMPARISON OF ADJUSTED AND UNADJUSTED USUAL
OCCUPATION STATISTICS FOR 1940*

KIND OF DATA	SKILLED OCCUPATIONS			SEMISKILLED OCCUPATIONS			UNSKILLED OCCUPATIONS		
	Whites	Non-Whites	Whites Divided by Non-Whites	Whites	Non-Whites	Whites Divided by Non-Whites	Whites	Non-Whites	Whites Divided by Non-Whites
Unadjusted statistics.	0.408	0.097	4.198	0.171	0.120	1.424	0.236	0.538	0.438
Adjusted statistics.	0.410	0.100	4.112	0.168	0.121	1.389	0.234	0.529	0.442

* Source: *Sample Statistics on Usual Occupations*, Table 4; and Edwards, *Comparative*, Table 2.

from the 1930 (and earlier) and the 1940 censuses are often not strictly comparable, even if the occupational titles are the same; he constructed occupational indexes which make it possible to compare 1940 with previous years.[21] In Table 18 the unadjusted and adjusted figures are compared. It is clear that the differences are small—less than 3 per cent for all categories. This suggests that only a small error results from using unadjusted data.

20. Males in the following occupations were misclassified: incorrectly classified as skilled: (1) factory painters (should have been semiskilled); incorrectly classified as semiskilled: (1) coopers (should have been skilled), (2) heaters (should have been unskilled), (3) blasters (should have been unskilled), (4) furnace men (should have been unskilled).

21. See Edwards, *Comparative*, Table 2.

c) 1930

Occupational data are found in the 1930 Census with a breakdown for sex and race.[22] The statistics in Table 12 are computed from data in Edwards' book.[23]

d) 1920

The statistics in Table 12 are computed from data in Edwards' book.[24] Since the 1920 Census was taken in January while others were taken in the spring, farm workers ten to fifteen years old seem to have been underestimated in 1920 as compared with other years. Edwards[25] estimated the undercount of male children to be 343,825. The total number of farm laborers was obtained by adding this number to the enumerated farm laborers. It was assumed that Negroes constituted the same proportion of the total number of farm laborers as they did of the enumerated number.

This change in census data may have introduced other biases, their amount depending on the kind of occupations for which the demand is relatively large in the spring or winter. It has been assumed here that the undercount of male farm laborers was the only bias introduced by the change in the enumeration date.[26]

e) 1910

Farm laborers were overestimated in the 1910 Census.[27] The adjusted number of Negroes was assumed to be the same proportion of the adjusted number of farm laborers as they were of the enumerated number.

22. U.S. Bureau of the Census, *Census of Population, 1930*, chap.vii, Table 2.

23. Edwards, *Socio-economic*, Tables 2 and 4.

24. *Ibid.*

25. *Comparative*, pp. 138–39.

26. Although Edwards added 388,461 additional males to the enumerated data (*ibid.*, pp. 140–41), I did not, because there does not seem to be much evidence supporting this adjustment.

27. U.S. Bureau of the Census, *Census of Population, 1910* (Washington, D.C.: Government Printing Office, 1914), Vol. V, Table 6; Edwards, *Socio-economic*, Tables 2 and 4. See Edwards, *Comparative*, pp. 137–38, for the derivation of this estimate.

f) 1900

Occupational statistics prior to 1910 were not so detailed or so accurate as those in later censuses.[28] However, by relying on Edwards' work,[29] it is possible to obtain statistics for 1890 and 1900 that are somewhat comparable to those for later years. To obtain comparability, it is necessary to combine unskilled and semiskilled occuptations into one category.

The data for 1900 give a breakdown for sex and race,[30] but many classifications combined occupations belonging to different skill categories. If at least 85 per cent of the workers in a classification were in the same skill category in 1910, all workers in this classification were allocated to this category. All other classifications were omitted from the calculations. Those omitted included "iron and steel workers," "metal workers," "other persons in trade and transportation," etc. The number of males in the omitted classifications was about 14 per cent of all gainfully occupied males (excluding farmers and farm tenants).

g) 1890

The data for 1890 give a breakdown for sex and race.[31] The same assumption was used to allocate classifications to different skill categories as for 1900. Once again, about 14 per cent of all gainfully occupied males (excluding farmers and farm tenants) were omitted.

There seems to have been an underenumeration of male farm laborers in 1890.[32] Again it was assumed that Negroes were the same proportion of total farm laborers as of enumerated farm laborers.

28. Edwards, *Comparative*, p. 88.

29. *Ibid.*, pp. 104–56.

30. U.S. Bureau of the Census, *Special Report on Occupations, 1900* (Washington, D.C.: Government Printing Office, 1904), Table 2.

31. U.S. Bureau of the Census, *Compendium, 1890* (Washington, D.C.: Government Printing Office, 1897), Table 78.

32. U.S. Bureau of the Census, *Census of Population, 1910*, pp. lxvi–lxxiii.

2. TABLE 15

a) *1950*

The 1950 statistics in Table 14 are for employed persons, and the 1950 statistics in Table 15 likewise refer to employed persons.[33]

b) *1940*

There is no regional breakdown of the data on usual occupations, but there are regional statistics giving the present occupations of employed persons and the last occupation of experienced unemployed;[34] these are used in Table 15. Table 17 shows that these statistics overestimate the relative number of skilled whites and underestimate the relative number of semiskilled whites. However, these biases are rather small and could not significantly change our interpretations.

c) *1910*

For 1910 there are data giving occupations by state, race, and sex,[35] but only the more important occupations within each state are reported. The figures for the South were obtained by adding together those for each southern state, and the figures for the North were obtained by subtracting the southern totals from those for the United States. It is very difficult to estimate precisely the number of individuals in the omitted occupations. Sample calculations suggest that from 4 to 8 per cent of the gainfully occupied males were omitted from the state statistics.

ADDENDUM TO CHAPTER 9

I tried to determine the secular trend during the first half of this century in the market discrimination against American Negroes. Since readily available income data before the late thirties were

33. U.S. Bureau of the Census, *Census of Population, 1950,* Table 159.

34. U.S. Bureau of the Census, *Census of Population, 1940,* Vol. III, Table 63.

35. U.S. Bureau of the Census, *Census of Population, 1910,* Table 7.

Addendum reprinted with minor changes from *Review of Economics and Statistics,* May 1962.

lacking, secular changes in occupational distributions were examined. A secular decline in discrimination probably occurred if there was a large increase in the relative number of Negroes in the more skilled and prized occupations. Data brought together for 1910, 1940, and 1950 clearly revealed that Negroes had significantly advanced their occupational position in both the North and South. The data also revealed, however, a significant advance by whites, and therefore, a qualitative examination of this evidence could not indicate whether Negroes had advanced more than whites. My problem paralleled many long-solved by economists with index numbers and by demographers and others with standardized averages. Outputs, prices, birth rates, etc., in different periods or areas are made comparable through aggregate indexes, which usually are fixed weighted averages of the individual components, as in a Laspeyres or Paasche index.[36] So I proceeded to construct "indexes of occupational position" for the different years, which were fixed weighted averages of the proportion of Negroes or whites in different skill categories, the weights being the relative wages paid to whites in 1939.

These occupational indexes seemed as relevant in determining the advance of Negroes as price and output indexes are in determining the advance of prices and outputs. Yet Professor Rayack takes vigorous exception, arguing that "There is . . . a serious error in Professor Becker's construction of an occupational index."[37] The "serious error" is simply that I used fixed weights instead of current year weights.[38] Would Professor Rayack also claim that there is a serious error in the BLS Consumer Price Index because it uses fixed

36. Sometimes several fixed weighted indexes are chained together into a single more complicated index.

37. Alton Rayack, "Discrimination and the Occupational Progress of Negroes," *Review of Economics and Statistics*, XVIII (May 1961), p. 210.

38. "His index employs *constant* weights of relative income for the three classes of skills and thus does not take into account the sharp narrowing of income differentials which has occurred since 1940. Since Negroes are much more heavily concentrated in semiskilled and unskilled occupations than are whites, the relative improvement of the Negroes is seriously understated when constant relative income weights are used." (*Ibid.*, 210.)

base year quantity weights instead of current year weights? I doubt it, for if current weights were used, the index would not measure movements in prices alone but that combined with movements in quantities. In the same way Rayack's indexes of occupational position—which use current year weights—do not measure entry into the more skilled occupations alone, but that combined with changes in earnings differentials. Perhaps this argument can be made clearer with an example. Suppose the relative number of Negroes and whites in different occupations remained absolutely constant over time. Surely an index which alleges to measure entry into skilled occupations should not show any change. The fixed-weighted indexes I used would not, while the weighted indexes preferred by Rayack would change whenever there was any change in earnings differentials.

It appears, therefore, that my indexes do and Rayack's do not correctly measure occupational position. His discussion does, however, indirectly raise the question of whether the patterns suggested by fixed-weighted indexes are very sensitive to the weights used. To test this I computed indexes using the 1951 weights derived by Rayack. The results, shown in the following table, strongly confirm those obtained with 1939 weights: both indicate little net change in the relative occupational position of Negroes from 1910 to 1950.

TABLE 18A

INDEX OF THE OCCUPATIONAL POSITION OF NEGROES AND
WHITES, 1910, 1940, AND 1950 (1951 WEIGHTS)

YEAR	NORTH			SOUTH		
	Whites	Negroes	Negroes Divided by Whites	Whites	Negroes	Negroes Divided by Whites
1950....	1.53	1.30	.85	1.52	1.21	.79
1940....	1.49	1.22	.82	1.45	1.13	.78
1910....	1.41	1.16	.82	1.33	1.08	.81

SOURCE: Rayack, op. cit., 210 and Table 15 in chapter 9 above.

So the impression of a rather striking stability in the relative occupational position of Negroes does not greatly depend on the weighting system used.

Since my study was concerned with the *overall* secular trend during the first half of the century, I did not pay much attention to changes within sub-periods. I now believe, however, that I was amiss in not pointing out that from the viewpoint of contemporary or future events a more sanguine interpretation might be given to the rise from 1940 to 1950. Although small by absolute standards, it is very large relative to the per decade change from 1910 to 1940. The year 1940 may have marked the turning point when Negroes began entering skilled occupations on a much larger scale than previously. It should be noted, though, that Negroes apparently advanced only slightly during the fifties.[39]

In conclusion, let me note that Rayack is wrong in suggesting[40] that there is an inconsistency between indexes showing a modest improvement in the occupational position of Negroes during the forties and indexes showing a large rise in their relative incomes. Indeed, their divergent movement only demonstrates again the advantage of a fixed-weighted occupational index, or more generally, of an index separating an advance into skilled occupations from other changes. His tables indicate that a good part of the income rise resulted from a general narrowing of earning differentials among occupations. Surely the presumed change in discrimination against Negroes is very different if their relative incomes rose because of their advance into skilled occupations than if they rose because relative earnings in unskilled occupations, where Negroes are heavily represented, rose.[41] The similarity between the movement in

39. Their relative occupational position in the country as a whole went from .816 in 1950 to .822 in 1958 (if 1951 weights are used). Rayack's occupational indexes declined during this period presumably because earnings differentials widened.

40. "Wage and salary income data for Negroes and whites also raise doubts concerning Becker's conclusion that the occupational position of Negroes relative to whites has changed little since 1940." (*Ibid.*, 211.)

41. Neither Rayack's nor my occupational indexes try to measure the effect

relative incomes and in Rayack's occupational index and the divergent movement shown by my index is not, therefore, testimony to the value of his and the error in mine (as alleged by Rayack) but, on the contrary, strikingly shows the advantage of a fixed-weighted index in discovering the sources of a change in relative incomes as well as in measuring occupational position.

---

of a rise in the relative incomes of Negroes *within* a given occupation (see my comment, in Chapter 9, n. 7).

CHAPTER TEN

Summary

1. THE MODEL

In this monograph a framework has been proposed for analyzing discrimination in the market place because of race, religion, sex, color, social class, personality, or other non-pecuniary considerations. Individuals are assumed to act as if they have "tastes for discrimination," and these tastes are the most important immediate cause of actual discrimination. When an employer discriminates against employees, he acts as if he incurs non-pecuniary, psychic costs of production by employing them; when an employee discriminates against fellow employees or employers, he acts as if he incurs non-pecuniary, psychic costs of employment by working with them; when a consumer discriminates against products, he acts as if he incurs non-pecuniary, psychic costs of consumption by consuming them.

It is desirable to formulate these non-pecuniary costs or tastes in a way that is sufficiently specific to yield quantitative empirical insights and sufficiently general to incorporate new information as it becomes available. Both these desiderata are satisfied by the concept of a "discrimination coefficient." The discrimination coefficient of an employer against an employee measures the value placed on the non-pecuniary cost of employing him, since it represents the percentage difference between the money and the true or net wage rate "paid" to him. If π is the money wage rate paid, then $\pi(1 + d)$ is the net wage rate, with d being the discrimination coefficient. Likewise, the discrimination coefficient of other employees against this employee measure the value placed on the non-pecuniary costs of working with him, since it represents the percentage difference between the money and the net wage rates received for working with him; and the discrimination coefficient of a consumer measures the value placed on the non-pecuniary costs of buying a product (partly) produced or sold by him, since it represents the percentage difference between the money and the net price paid for this product.

Although these coefficients are the proximate determinant of choices, they are in turn, like other tastes, influenced by more fundamental variables. In the past, those who attempted to establish a relation between discrimination and other variables usually employed rather direct techniques, as exemplified by the interpretation of answers to questionnaires. By relating discrimination coefficients to an economic analysis of price determination through the market mechanism, it is possible to infer indirectly some of these relationships from data giving incomes and other economic statistics for various groups. These inferences are usually restricted to whites and Negroes or whites and non-whites because data are lacking for other groups.

2. TASTES FOR DISCRIMINATION

Since people discriminate little against those with whom they have only indirect "contact" in the market place, some direct contact must be necessary for the development of a desire to discriminate. This does not necessarily contradict the view that discrimination would be eliminated if people got to know one another sufficiently well through close contact. It merely emphasizes that, while certain kinds of contact may be a cure for discrimination, others may cause it. Several different kinds of contact were examined in an attempt to discover the most important ones.

Discrimination against Negroes seems to be positively correlated with their relative number. However, this relation is stronger for discrimination that does not go through the market (as illustrated by opportunities for formal education) than for discrimination that does. Moreover, while this relation can be measured in various ways, e.g., by using the relative number of Negroes in a plant, firm, city, or state, their (relative) number in a metropolitan area is the only one used in this study. The amount of contact between Negroes and whites can be measured not only by the relative numerical importance of Negroes but also by their relative economic importance. Various measures of economic importance were suggested, but it was not possible here to investigate any of them carefully.

Contact has other dimensions besides numerical and economic importance; among them are intensity, duration, and "level." There is some evidence that discrimination is less against Negroes in temporary than in permanent jobs, and this may occur because the duration of contact is less. There is also abundant evidence that discrimination by Negroes against one another is much less than is discrimination by whites against Negroes, and this may result from the more intense contact among Negroes (and among whites) than between Negroes and whites. Intense contact can be associated with little discrimination for at least three reasons: (1) discrimination may be caused by ignorance, and contact may eliminate this ignorance; (2) Negroes and whites may have different physical and social characteristics, and contact may lead Negroes and whites to value their own characteristics; (3) Negroes may discriminate less and have more contact with one another precisely because they value their own characteristics.

Evidence clearly shows that discrimination is greater against older and better-educated non-whites. (This does not imply that older and better-educated whites discriminate more than those who are younger and less educated; none of the evidence examined has any direct bearing on this.) This greater discrimination may reflect, at least partly, a positive connection between discrimination and occupation, since older and better-educated non-whites have higher and more responsible occupational positions. Whites in lower occupations may greatly discriminate against them because they have a relatively large amount of authority and decision-making powers. Data showing the incomes of whites and non-whites in different occupations are extremely limited, but the crude evidence available does not contradict this hypothesis. An alternative, albeit related, interpretation is that discrimination is greater against older and better-educated non-whites because their income is large relative to the persons with whom they are employed. This interpretation emphasizes that the level of contact can also be measured by income, and discrimination by whites may be a decreasing function of their income relative to non-whites. It has been impossible to determine whether either relation between discrimination and "level" of contact is an important explanation of the increase in discrimination with age and education.

Within each region members of the same economic factor of production appear to have very similar tastes for discrimination; however, the reader should be cautious in accepting this conclusion, since the statistical procedures used probably overestimated this similarity.

In the last few decades much controversy and legislation have centered around regional differences in discrimination against Negroes and other non-whites. By developing an analysis based on the concept of a discrimination coefficient, it was possible to make the first quantitative estimate of such regional differences. In 1940, tastes for discrimination in the South appear to have been, on the average, about twice those in the North. Although relatively more Negroes live in the South, this does not seem to explain much of the regional difference in discrimination, nor can other variables examined explain this difference, and at present it must be accepted as reflecting a regional difference in tastes.

How has the absolute and relative economic position of Negroes changed over time? Insight into this was obtained by examining the occupational position of Negroes and whites for several dates during the last half-century. The average occupational position of Negroes has risen quite strikingly in both the North and the South, but their position relative to whites has been remarkably stable; in the North this was only slightly higher in 1950 than in 1910, and in the South it was slightly lower in 1950 than in 1910. While many important and relevant changes may have taken place in both regions, a very tentative conclusion from this stability would be that neither striking increases nor striking decreases in discrimination against Negroes have occurred during the last four decades.

3. MARKET DISCRIMINATION AND SEGREGATION

Tastes for discrimination are an important part of the theory explaining actual discrimination, but there is no simple and unique way to go from one to the other. The theory incorporates an analysis of other variables which, so to speak, determine the observable form taken by tastes. Suppose one is interested in members of two groups, called N and W, respectively. Tastes for discrimination affect market relationships by causing market discrimination or market segregation or both against N or W.

Market discrimination against N exists if discrimination has reduced N's average net wage rate (or income) by a greater percentage than W's; the *market discrimination coefficient* (MDC) is defined as the difference between the actual ratio of W's average net wage rate (or income) to N's and the ratio that would exist if there were no discrimination. The MDC equals zero if there is no discrimination and is an increasing function of the amount of market discrimination against N. If N and W are perfect substitutes in production and if there is perfect competition in all markets, the MDC is simply the percentage difference between W's and N's actual average net wage rates (or incomes). Market segregation of members of N exists if they have more contact with one another than they would have if there were no discrimination; a *market segregation coefficient* (MSC) could be defined as the difference between a measure of actual contact and what it would be if there were no segregation. It is easy to confuse these two concepts, and yet a careful distinction between market segregation and market discrimination is essential for a clear understanding of the observable consequences of tastes for discrimination.

Market discrimination was analyzed in individual labor and capital markets and in all markets combined. The latter analysis employed a model in which members of W and N owned various quantities of two homogeneous factors of production—labor and capital. Effective discrimination occurred against N if discrimination by either W or N reduced N's total net (i.e., net of psychic costs) income by a greater percentage than W's. By abstracting from government discrimination and monopolistic practices, it is possible completely to isolate the structural forces causing effective discrimination in a competitive economy.

Discrimination must decrease the total net incomes of both N and W; it decreases N's total net income by a greater percentage than W's if

$$\frac{Y_w}{Y_n} > \frac{l_n}{l_w},$$

where Y_n and Y_w are the aggregate incomes of N and W when there is no discrimination, and l_n and l_w are the amounts of labor supplied by N and W. Thus effective discrimination would occur against N if W was more of an "economic majority" than N was a "labor majority." This inequality is necessary as well as sufficient if W alone discriminates but is not necessary if N also does. Political discrimination is often strongest against political minorities, and this result shows that economic discrimination is strongest against economic minorities.

It was also shown that if $l_n < l_w$ and if N is relatively well supplied with labor, effective discrimination must occur against N. This explains, for example, why Negroes in the United States suffer more than whites from discrimination: even without monopolies, trade unions, and government discrimination, substantial discrimination by whites (and a fortiori by Negroes) would greatly reduce the net income of Negroes.

The MDC against members of N selling a particular kind of labor (or capital) clearly depends on the average tastes for discrimination of all groups—factors of production, employers, and consumers—working with N in the market place. However, it does not depend on this alone. A given taste for discrimination causes more market discrimination if the group is complementary to, rather than substitutable for, N, so that the distribution of tastes between substitutes and complements is important.

Differences among members of the same group may also be important. At each equilibrium position, some members of a group work with N and others with members of W that are selling the same labor (or capital); it is easy to show that those working with N have relatively small discrimination coefficients against N. An increase in the supply of N relative to W means that some of those working with W must be induced to work with N; since they have relatively large discrimination coefficients, they can be induced to do so only if the relative return for working with N increases, and an increase in this relative return must be accompanied by an increase in the MDC against N. Therefore, the MDC changes with all changes in the relative supply of N if there are differences in tastes within a group. As mentioned earlier, however, the evidence suggests that members of the same group usually have very similar tastes for discrimination against non-whites.

The extent of concentration in the labor and output markets is also relevant to the extent of discrimination. Employer discrimination should, on the average, be less in competitive industries than in monopolistic ones. Monopolistic and competitive industries in the South were investigated for 1940. For all eight census occupational categories, the number of non-whites employed by monopolistic industries relative to the number employed by competitive industries is quite consistent with our theory. Another theoretical implication is that employee discrimination is larger in unionized than in equivalent competitive labor markets, but the relevant empirical material has not been examined.

The analysis developed in this monograph implies—for fixed discrimination coefficients—a negative correlation between the market discrimination against N and N's relative economic importance in the productive process. All the evidence examined is consistent with this implication. For example, Negroes tend to be more numerous in occupations and industries in which they have relatively little contact with whites.

Segregation of (say) Negroes and whites occurs because Negroes want to discriminate less against other Negroes than whites do; some segregation is found throughout our social and economic system. Complete market segregation does not occur because the relative supply of factors owned by Negroes and whites differs, making it profitable for Negroes to "trade" with whites, even though there is substantial discrimination against them. As mentioned earlier, segregation and discrimination are often confused, and a good example of this confusion is found in the discussions of Negro housing.

Many whites do not want to live near Negroes, and this is a primary cause of residential segregation, not of residential discrimination (as is often believed). The latter could occur only if many whites were willing to forfeit income in order to avoid renting or selling a dwelling to Negroes who would live near *other* whites. My own conjecture is that this kind of behavior is not very common and that the residential discrimination observed in many northern cities is a consequence of the in-migration of Negroes and the residential segregation in these cities.

Differentials between whites and non-whites have been explained in terms of discrimination against non-whites, although a theory based on nepotism in favor of whites would have almost exactly the same empirical implications. In other words a theory based on "hatred" of one group is not easily distinguished empirically from one based on "love" of the other group. Thus these two theories can be used interchangeably for most problems in positive economic analysis; at the same time, one's conclusions about normative issues may greatly depend on whether "hatred" or "love" is assumed to motivate decisions.

4. SUGGESTIONS FOR FUTURE RESEARCH

Since the theroretical framework proposed in this monograph seems consistent with both general knowledge and the available quantitative evidence, it may not be amiss to point out some implications that can fruitfully be investigated further. Additional analysis of differentials between whites and non-whites would be worthwhile, since data are relatively abundant and discrimination against non-whites is currently a very pressing issue. The large regional difference in discrimination in 1940 could not be explained by the regional distribution of non-whites. The 1950 Census data should be subjected to a similar analysis; if like conclusions are reached, an attempt should be made to discover variables that can account for the difference. It would also be interesting to determine whether the traditionally greater unemployment of non-whites than of whites is consistent with the analysis presented here.

Studies should be made of the relative importance of employer, employee, consumer, and government discrimination. One study could extend this work on the relative amount of employer discrimination in monopolistic and competitive industries; another could investigate the relative amount of employee discrimination in unionized and competitive labor markets. The latter would probably be especially fruitful, since too often the word has been taken for the deed; that is, union pronouncements have been considered synonymous with union behavior.

Data from the 1950 Census could be used to determine the scope, magnitude, and causes of segregation and discrimination in housing. The literature on minority housing is sufficiently confused to make this an extremely promising field.

A more thorough study should be made of the relation between market discrimination against a group of non-whites and their importance in the productive process. This relation has not previously received much attention in the literature.

There is abundant evidence that discrimination against non-whites systematically increases with their age and education. Many barriers to the education of non-whites will probably be taken down in the future, and this will increase their education relative to that of whites. This would also increase their income relative to that of whites if there were no discrimination; but, since discrimination rises with education, an increase in the education of non-whites may increase only slightly their incomes relative to those of whites. Hence it is important to investigate the cause of the greater market discrimination against older and better-educated non-whites.

The power of the analysis can be further tested by applying it to other groups, such as women, Jews, individuals with the same personality type, members of the same caste or social class, etc. Data limitations preclude a detailed study of most of the groups except women, for whom there is a large quantity of economic information. An analysis of income and occupational differentials between men and women should be very useful not only because much discrimination has occurred against women but also because it has long been recognized that "productivity" differences between men and women explain a significant part of these differentials. Discussions of other minorities usually reveal an unwillingness to admit that important differences in "productivity" and "taste" exist between them and the majority. I believe that these differences *are* important, although the discussion in this monograph is probably also biased toward underestimating them. An analysis of the relative returns to women should therefore add some perspective to discussions of discrimination against all minorities.

The analysis in this monograph can be viewed as a case study in the quantitative analysis of non-pecuniary variables. In recent years much emphasis has been placed on the importance of non-pecuniary variables in the choice of occupation, working conditions, etc.; yet little has been done toward *estimating* their quantitative importance. The present analysis of discrimination suggests a quantitative approach to these other non-pecuniary variables, and this may be its most useful by-product.

Index